Old Europe

Stop The Great Replacement!

By

Rikard Högberg

LEGATUM PUBLISHING
Identity · History · Knowledge

2022

Original:
Old Europe Shame On You!
Democratic Demographic Institute, 2002

Scientific research: Mikhail Khomin
Art editor: Alex Kaluzhnov
Cover design: Alex Kaluzhnov
Illustrations: Rikard Högberg
Proofreading & comments: Christopher Pascone

Title:
Old Europe Stop The Great Replacement.

Author: Rikard Högberg

ISBN **978-82-93925-11-8**
2nd paperback edition

BIC classification: SOCIOLOGY & ANTHROPOLOGY (JH),
Population & demography (JHBD)

Cover: Legatum Publishing
Editor: Bjørn Christian Rødal
Layout: Richard Krogstad

LEGATUM PUBLISHING AS
www.legatum-publishing.com

This book acknowledges the fact that every family needs 2.1 children, two to replace you and your partner and 0.1 per couple to cover up for those not having any children.

European families have, on average, 1.5 children.

Foreword

I wrote the first edition in 2002. This updated 2nd edition has new and recent statistics. We left the original numbers for comparison. They give an honest and alarming view of how fast it is going in the wrong direction.

The second edition has some extra chapters with information collected recently.

A vile replacement policy is being promoted by the globalist ruling class that governs our countries. They rule through false and misleading information and propaganda, rigged elections, threats and even assassinations, or so-called suicides when it suits them. Globalist actors, such as George Soros and Bill Gates, fund and direct obedient corporations and NGOs that do whatever they wish. Their actions all point in one direction; they want to destroy Europe. They want to replace the European population and independence with a new and easily manipulated low-wage slave population.

They want to destroy people making innovations that could threaten their hegemony.

They hate independent-minded people. They hate intelligent people who can think for themselves. They hate people they cannot bribe. And by extension, as a European, they hate you. They want you extinct and gone. Thus the falling birthrates in Western countries is not a slump. It is the direct result of enacted policies perpetrated by our countries' currently most potent elements. They fund demographic institutes and "think tanks" that come up with these replacement immigration policies.

On top of this, millions of tons of pollution that diminish sperm quality are poured into our ecosystem every year from the industries owned and controlled by the same globalist ruling class.

But there is a significant change coming. This will be the biggest change in the history of the world. Fewer and fewer people are reading mainstream media that are owned by globalists. The United States Supreme Court has decided to remove Roe Versus Wade. This will raise the number of children in the USA and influence decisions worldwide. The petrodollar will collapse and be replaced by gold-based sovereign currencies worldwide. That means that the global finance and banking system will change drastically, eliminating a vast parasitic burden on our economies worldwide and leading to increased freedom and prosperity in our nations. In history, we see that in the periods when cultures and countries had sovereignty, and their currency was linked to gold, the economy bloomed.

CNN has lost 90% of its viewers by lying to them for decades. CNN+ had to be closed down after only two months and a more than 400 million USD loss. The alternative media now serves the majority of the news in the USA. People understand that Twitter has more than 20% bots and fake accounts to guide you to do what the globalists want. Muhammed Bin Salman has taken over the ownership of Google, Facebook and Instagram from the globalist Alwaleed bin Talal. This will make a considerable change.

Kicking out the illegal aliens from Martha's Vineyard (USA) made the moral collapse of the Globalist left clear for the whole world to see.

The liberal elite showed its face with how they reacted when illegal aliens were dropped off into the middle of their little globalist-left haven. Globalist-Leftist political and media demagogues everywhere were melting down over the situation. This situation illustrated very clearly for the whole world to see that there is one set of rules for us, the average man in the street, and another for them. They welcome immigrants and refugees if they do not have to live next to these immigrants.

The real message is to be understood from their outrage. It shows just how duplicitous and shameless the globalist left is as they attempt to shield themselves against any intrusion by removing themselves to remote and walled-off places; while demanding everyone else make sacrifices "for the greater good" and live in fear; to tolerate increasing crime and decreasing quality of life.

The lion's share of the population in the USA, and many other parts of the world, now realise the hypocrisy of the Globalist-left. They have nothing left but to squall as stuck pigs.

And with this moral collapse, the "great" replacement has come under scrutiny and will eventually be stopped.

Since the millennial shift in 2000, when I wrote the book "Old Europe Shame on You" in English and Russian, which was written to increase the Russian birth rate, it has now risen from 1.7 per woman to 1.8 per woman in Russia. Through the Hungarian Department of Foreign Affairs, I have also contributed to the effort to increase the Hungarian population. Prime Minister Victor Orban and his advisors have done a winsome, fulsome and excellent job of increasing the Hungarian population.

Now my next goal is to increase the Norwegian population of Norwegians born in Norway to 10 million people! Make children! Wake people up! Do your research and think for yourself! Be happy! Be kind!

Rikard Högberg

Stockholm, August 2022

These empires failed due to complacency and decadence:

The Etruscan culture, The Abbasid caliphate, The Mughal Empire,

The Roman Empire, and The Ottoman Empire.

They were all overcome by a more virile rival,

and Europe is next on the chopping block if we do not take heed!

Table of Contents

Illustrations and Tables

Introduction

I have written this book to point out the enormous societal changes that are taking place but are hardly even acknowledged or seriously analysed by most Western media outlets, especially in Old Europe.

This book foresees a dramatic change in economics and the upheaval of Western regimes. History shows that such changes have taken place many times before. We are not educated on this, and as a result, we do not remember our account.

There is a coming conflict on the horizon that will overturn Western democracy, following the pattern of democracies that have gone extinct before.

This book also concludes, much to the chagrin of the politically correct, that some people are more intelligent than others. But these people tend to become overly individualistic and ego-focused and therefore die out. To ensure continued high economic production, individualistic societies such as Germany and France attempt to import and absorb skilled foreign workers because their own native populations do not make enough children. However, this is easier said than done.

War, however, rather than a slow-burning societal conflict that we are currently mired in right now, drives up the birth rate dramatically. Just look at what happened in Europe in the 1940s, right after the war was concluded. The big "baby boom" spread all over Europe and America. This "baby-boomer" generation has reached pension age, but there aren't enough people in the next generation to replace them in the workforce.

Western economies will suffer substantially. Old Europe's high standard of living will fall to pieces. Because we turned our demographic base upside down, there will be a majority of older people and a minority of young people. Our current trend leads to economic collapse in Old Europe, and new economies in the world will take over. It is of the utmost importance to ask how to remedy this, or at the very least, how to survive the coming conflict and collapse.

Forget the old textbooks such as Philip Kotler's works; they are shortsighted, showing only short-term economic thinking, designed only for private business executives, not politicians and long-term state policy. Forget the Nobel Prize in economics. The Nobel Prize only reflects a myopic worldview. The whole economic discipline is infected by reductionistic and short-term thinking.

This book predicts that the Western world will disappear, especially Old Europe, if we do not change our ways.

1. The bitter Fight

What can you do to save the Western world? How can you help your society and safeguard the hard-won freedoms inherited from our ancestors?

You can raise awareness of the problem of falling birth rates. Even more importantly, you can help families with many children — or even better, have children yourself.

Our birth rates all over the west have been declining for a long time now. The decline in birth rates has happened in lockstep with our modernisation and economic development, especially as we have, on average, gained more years of higher education. There is a linear inverse relationship between the amount of education a person has and the number of children they have[1] (the more years of education, the less likely they are to have children).

However, being well educated should be the opposite; you should have many children. Our aim should be to reverse this trend and encourage highly educated, intelligent, and high-income earners to have many children. More years of education should lead to more children. Before the advent of the welfare state, this was usually the case. People with more resources and higher levels of education could afford to have more children. Almost everyone can afford to have children now, but most choose to postpone it until the end of their fertile years.

The problem we face is, first and foremost, not an economic question but a cultural one. It is a question of cultural prestige. At the same time, economic policies that compensate young women for postponing their education in favour of having children while in their younger fertile years is a reasonable short-term fix; meanwhile, we are addressing the bigger cultural question. Such compensation could be you get several years of free education per child or debt forgiveness and tax cuts like in Hungary; any female who owes a student debt will have her outstanding balance cut by

[1] Janowitz, Barbara S. "An Analysis of the Impact of Education on Family Size." Demography 13, no. 2 (1976): 189–98. https://doi.org/10.2307/2060800. (Accessed 11.07.22)

50% if she gives birth to 2 children. With three children or more, her student debt will be forgiven, according to Hungarian Free Press[2].

Support for women studying in universities to have children is especially important because it is in her early twenties that a woman is most fertile, not at the age of thirty (which is the average age of a woman having her first child in Stockholm, Sweden). Education and career building usually last until a woman is forty years old in Europe, but by then, it's usually too late in the biological sense to bear children. Those who try anyway and are successful may have only one or two kids.

Regarding the cultural question, you can share some of your time and resources to help those close to you, especially younger fertile members of your family and the local community. You can help your friends and relatives by helping them to raise children. You can share your time, knowledge, and wisdom, letting young people know they will not be alone with the daunting task of childrearing.

It is hard work, we know, but it is worth it.

Having children with wholesome values and empathy is the best guarantee of peace and the long-term survival of your society.

Simply sending money to some charitable organisation is just a way to ease your bad conscience. The only person on your mind is still you, and by giving away money, you ease the "bad feeling" for a while, but ultimately this doesn't work. It just postpones the problem of bearing too little responsibility for the society you live in and creates the illusion that sending money to the "Third World" will solve problems. A much more real and concrete contribution to the world is to engage with the actual people around you, where you live.

---

[2] Adam, Christopher. 2017. Hungarian action plan seeks to dramatically increase birth rate by 2030. [https://hungarianfreepress.com/2017/05/25/hungarian-action-plan-seeks-to-dramatically-increase-birth-rate-by-2030/] (Accessed 11.07.22)

2. World population today and tomorrow

Today, the world population consists of about 6 billion people. Within 50 years, this number will possibly be between 9-12 billion.

Already when this second edition is written, in July 2022, we are 7,9 billion people, according to Worldometers.[3]

We can see the Population Reference Bureau estimation below (one of the most respected population-measuring organisations in the world). From the graph, you see that in the year 2050, India will have the largest population in the world, but Congo, Ethiopia, and Nigeria will also climb the list.

The so-called developed countries will diminish and be superseded by the so-called developing countries. Europe and Japan will slowly die off, and Africa will prevail.

This impact contradicts the current perception of developing and developed countries. In such a world, you could say that the more developed a country, the sooner it dies out.

This graph tells us that developed or industrial countries are diminishing countries. A significant country in the future will be India, which is currently the largest democratic country in the world. After implementing Western economic standards, India will be one of the world's leading countries.

Within 50 years of the current trend, Germany will have died out. Russia will have to increase its population to 300 million just to keep the same rank it has now.

---

[3] Worldometers.info [https://www.worldometers.info/world-population/] (Accessed 11.07.22)

The World's Largest Countries In 2002 and 2022

Rank	Country[4]	Population (millions)	Country[3]	Pop. 2022 (millions)
1	China	1,281	China	1,451
2	India	1,050	India	1,409
3	USA	287	USA	335
4	Indonesia	217	Indonesia	280
5	Brazil	174	Pakistan	230
6	Russia	144	Brazil	216
7	Pakistan	144	Nigeria	218
8	Bangladesh	134	Bangladesh	168
9	Nigeria	130	Russia	146
10	Japan	127	Mexico	132
11	Mexico	102	Japan	126
12	Germany	82	Ethiopia	121
13	Philippines	80	Philippines	113
14	Vietnam	80	Egypt	107
15	Egypt	71	Vietnam	99

Table 1: 2003 predictions[4]

---

[4] The World Bank. [https://data.worldbank.org/indicator/SP.POP.TOTL] (Accessed 11.07.22)

The World's Largest Countries In 2002 and 2022

Rank	Country[3]	Estimate (millions)	Country[4]	Est. 2022 (millions)
1	India	1,628	India	1,639
2	China	1,394	China	1,402
3	USA	413	Nigeria	401
4	Pakistan	332	USA	379
5	Indonesia	316	Pakistan	338
6	Nigeria	304	Indonesia	331
7	Brazil	247	Brazil	229
8	Bangladesh	205	Ethiopia	205
9	Congo	182	Congo	194
10	Ethiopia	173	Bangladesh	193
11	Mexico	154	Egypt	160
12	Philippines	146	Mexico	155
13	Vietnam	117	Philippines	144
14	Egypt	115	Russia	136
15	Russia	102	Tanzania	129

Table 2: World's Largest Countries in 2050, from 2003 and August 2022.

Table: UN World population prediction

World: Total Population

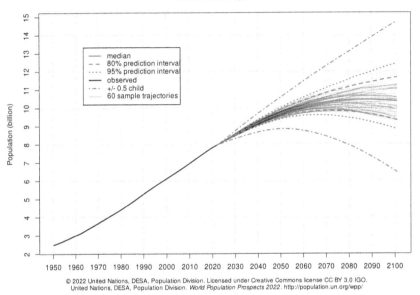

Ill. 1: Estimated World total population[5].

[5] United Nations, DESA, Population Division. World Population Prospects 2022. [https://population.un.org/wpp/Graphs/Probabilistic/POP/TOT/900] (Accessed 11.07.22)

Rankings of the world's ten most populous countries, 1990 and 2022, and medium scenario, 2050 (numbers in parentheses refer to total population in millions)

Rankings of the world's ten most populous countries

1990	2022	2050
China (1,144)	China (1,426)	India (1,668)
India (861)	India (1,412)	China (1,317)
United States of America (246)	United States of America (337)	United States of America (375)
Indonesia (181)	Indonesia (275)	Nigeria (375)
Brazil (149)	Pakistan (234)	Pakistan (366)
Russian Federation (148)	Nigeria (216)	Indonesia (317)
Japan (123)	Brazil (215)	Brazil (231)
Pakistan (114)	Bangladesh (170)	Dem. Republic of the Congo (215)
Bangladesh (106)	Russian Federation (145)	Ethiopia (213)
Nigeria (94)	Mexico (127)	Bangladesh (204)
Mexico (81)	Japan (124)	Mexico (144)
	Ethiopia (123)	Russian Federation (133)
	Dem. Republic of the Congo (97)	

Ill. 2: Rankings of the world's ten most populous countries

Note: The figure above depicts only countries among the ten most populous in 1990, 2022 or 2050. A blue arrow indicates a country maintaining the same rank, a yellow arrow indicates increased rank, and a green arrow indicates a declining position. The ten highest ranking countries are printed in black. Other countries are illustrated in grey. From United Nations[6]

[6] United Nations Department of Economic and Social Affairs, Population Division (2022). World Population. Prospects 2022: Summary of Results. UN DESA/POP/2022/TR/NO. 3. [https://www.un.org/development/desa/pd/sites/www.un.org.development.desa.pd/files/wpp2022_summary_of_results.pdf] (Accessed 11.07.22)

Western population in the world:

2002: 15%

2050: 5%

Percentage of population aged 65 years or over for the world, SDG regions, and selected groups of countries, 2022, 2030 and 2050, according to the medium scenario

Population of the world, SDG reg. and sel. countries

Region	2022	2030	2050
World	9.7	11.7	16.4
Sub-Saharan Africa	3.0	3.3	4.7
Northern Africa and Western Asia	5.5	7.0	12.5
Central and Southern Asia	6.4	8.1	13.4
Eastern and South-Eastern Asia	12.7	16.3	25.7
Latin America and the Caribbean	9.1	11.5	18.8
Australia/New Zealand	16.6	19.4	23.7
Oceania*	3.9	5.1	8.2
Europe and Northern America	18.7	22.0	26.9
Least developed countries	3.6	4.1	6.1
Landlocked developing countries (LLDC)	3.6	4.1	5.8
Small island developing States (SIDS)	8.9	11.3	16.0

*excluding Australia and New Zealand

Table 3: Population of the world, SDG reg. and sel. countries[7]

---

[7] United Nations Department of Economic and Social Affairs, Population Division (2022). World Population. Prospects 2022: Summary of Results. UN DESA/POP/2022/TR/NO. 3.
[https://www.un.org/development/desa/pd/sites/www.un.org.development.desa.pd/files/wpp2022_summary_of_results.pdf] (Accessed 11.07.22)

3. The western demographic situation

Europe

Europe is already Old Europe and dying of old age, apathy and cultural exhaustion. There is no sign of long-term recovery in the European economy or cultural revival. Europe is losing its traditions and its vision and excitement for the future. Complacency and apathy are spreading into more population groups. Relatively small clusters of financially and politically connected people enjoy great wealth by robbing the pensions of future Europeans in every country. The ageing of Europe makes political leaders and leading personalities even more stubborn and ego focused.

European politicians have neglected the demographic problem for many years. Europe is in terrible shape and is on its way to liquidation. Europeans have become spoiled and are hung over on cheap credit and consumerism. They live in such devastating abundance that, according to our theory, this abundance leads directly to the decadence and downfall of European culture.

Investments in the population are not sufficient. The growth rate of Europe's population is about 1.5 (2020) children per woman when it should be at least 2.1 to sustain itself (Recent numbers for 2020 show a birth rate of 1.5 for Europe[8]).

We do not invest enough in future generations. Pension systems in Europe are enormous "pyramid games" organised by greedy politicians to fuel money from pension funds into political reforms and policies, which keep these politicians in power. Journalists are too narrow-minded to react and are more interested in their petty concerns rather than being the far-sighted watchdogs they should be.

Europe will be one of the frontlines in the conflict to come. Europe will suffer the most from demographic changes. The EU is an enormous bribe

---

[8] Population Reference Bureau. 2021.
[https://www.prb.org/wp-content/uploads/2021/08/letter-booklet-2021-world-population.pdf] (Accessed 11.07.22)

machine[9][10][11] that will continue to hinder real development until a non-corrupt system has taken its place. It's unlikely that the EU will deal with its demographic problems. Europe has no 20-year vision or longer, only a two-to-four-year horizon. The European economy will fall until the European population again holds wholesome values and starts to grow.

If the population doesn't grow, Europe will fall into a new Dark Age for about 200 years, according to Professor Alexander Tytler's theory[12] (see graph, page 46).

Japan

The Japanese economy is dragging. An oligarchy is holding on to its power by all means. All attempts to clean up corrupt and backwards practices are met by a wall of professional naysayers - the men of the Old Guard.

The natural solution is to wait for a new generation to come into power, but such a generation is currently absent. With a birth rate of 1.3 (2020) instead of 2.1, it is apparent that the Japanese economy will not recover. It will experience small ups and downs, but until Japanese leadership has

---

[9] Turkey's $6.6 billion EU Bribe. 2016. The European Union Times – Breaking News, Latest News. [https://www.eutimes.net/2016/03/turkeys-6-6-billion-eu-bribe/] (Accessed 11.07.22)

[10] Boffey, Daniel. 2021. One in five people in parts of EU pay bribes for healthcare, survey finds; Corruption report says third of EU residents used personal connections to access care during Covid crisis. Guardian News & Media Limited. [https://www.theguardian.com/world/2021/jun/15/one-in-five-people-in-parts-of-eu-pay-bribes-for-healthcare-survey-finds] (Accessed 11.07.22)

[11] PRESS RELEASE No 9/2022. On 27 and 28 June, the European Anti-Fraud Office (OLAF) and its African partners met in Brussels to discuss how to strengthen cooperation in the fight against fraud and corruption. European Commission website. [https://anti-fraud.ec.europa.eu/media-corner/news/olaf-meets-african-partners-strengthen-eu-africa-cooperation-fighting-fraud-eu-budget-2022-06-28_en] (Accessed 11.07.22)

[12] North, Gary. 2019. The Mythical Alexander Tytler and His Theory of Democracy. GaryNorth.com, Inc. [https://www.garynorth.com/public/19505.cfm] (Accessed 27.07.22)

solved their demographic problem, there will be enormous problems in Japanese society.

Newly elected Japanese politicians do not have enough power to solve the demographic problem. Political leaders have to oust the old oligarchy from its ancient throne. The US occupation instituted an oligarchy after WW2. To oust this oligarchy is currently impossible. But there are some bright spots on the horizon with the newly elected (2022) Kamiya Sohei from the Sanseitō party (Party of Do it Yourself[13]), to the upper house. It shows a political awareness in Japan of these social, economic and demographic problems plaguing the developed world.

There is no reliable pension system in Japan. The country's public and private pension systems face severe problems because of the nation's rapidly ageing population. However, they are better constituted to meet this problem than Europe due to its homogenous population and culture of individual sacrifice for the greater societal good.

The Institute of Population Problems at the Japanese Ministry of Health and Welfare estimates that the number of people 65 and older will nearly be doubled in 2020, reaching 36.4 million. Senior citizens comprise about 29% of Japan's population[14], the highest proportion among all major industrial countries.

Japan's private sector pension system is facing severe strains because of too few corporate workers and too many retirees, implemented many rules based on economic conditions 30 years ago.

Many major Japanese companies are pushing for further deregulation in the structure and management of pension programs.

---

[13] Ryall , Julian. 2022. What's behind the rise of Japan's Sanseito, a far-right party that loves Trump and hates immigration? South China Morning Post Publishers Ltd. [https://www.scmp.com/week-asia/politics/article/3186275/whats-behind-rise-japans-sanseito-far-right-trump-loving-anti] (Accessed 27.07.22)

[14] Seniors account for record 29.1% of Japan's population. 2021. Kyodo News. [https://english.kyodonews.net/news/2021/09/e8d7087c9447-seniors-account-for-record-291-of-japans-population.html] (Accessed 27.07.22)

Japan's only approved corporate pension system is a defined-benefit program, where a company promises a certain level of future pension benefits. Because the return on investment has been low and the number of retirees has been rising, it has forced companies to increase pension plan contributions. Arguing the continued increase in donations could hurt a company's international competitiveness, business organisations, including the Japanese Federation of Employers' Associations, have begun to demand that the government ease or abolish various restrictions.

Japan has two basic corporate pension schemes:

1. Employee pension funds.

These funds manage and pay a part of what would otherwise be paid by public pension insurance. There were nearly 1,900 such funds in Japan, with an enrolment of about 12.1 million people as of March 1996. Assets in these funds added up to 41.6 trillion yen.

2. Tax-qualified pensions.

Unlike employee pension funds managed by outside organisations, tax-qualified pensions are managed by companies in-house.

These pensions are also completely separated from the public pension insurance system. These assets totalled about 17.8 trillion yen, with about 10.7 million members enrolled from 91,000 companies at the end of March 1996.

At retirement, employees usually are paid pensions in one of three ways: lump sum, annuity, or a combination of the first two.

The typical severance payment for a male worker with 30 years of service in a company with between 300 and 999 employees is about 15.35 million yen (about $139,000 at a dollar/yen exchange rate of 110/1). Source: 1992 Survey on Corporate Welfare Programs (Life Insurance Culture Centre).

Japanese journalists are afraid to fight with old power groups to make much-needed reforms. Japan will fall into a Cinderella sleep. If they are not vigilant in the coming years, Japanese culture will slowly fade away; Hawaiians and Turks will do Sumo wrestling.

USA

The USA is also struggling; 2020 numbers show the US birth rate has fallen from 2.1 in the previous version of the book, down to slightly below 1.8. There has been a serious decline in the birthrate over the last decades.

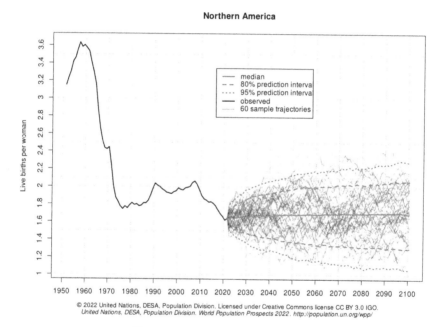

Ill. 3: Projections of Total Fertility USA[15]

Note: Probabilistic Projections of Total Fertility using fertility estimates. Projections of Total Fertility: Median, 80% / 95% prediction intervals.

---

[15] World Population Prospects. United Nations. [https://population.un.org/wpp/ Graphs/Probabilistic/FERT/TOT/905] (Accessed 19.10.22)

In the early 2000s, after the fall of the Soviet Union, the USA lost their global rival and ideological competitor. At first, this gave the USA an enormous boost in self-confidence, and they experienced what has become known as the unipolar moment. Francis Fukuyama famously called the US victory in the cold war the "End of History". In the 1990's it looked like it was going to become the American century. For the first time in history, they were unopposed and could dictate freely and do as they pleased without meaningful opposition. Most excitement had worn off at the end of the 90s and early 2000s, and signs of exhaustion had settled in. Without a rival or an external threat, the US population had meagre incentives to unify and push forward. Then 9/11 happened, and the new spectre of terrorism emerged. It gave the USA temporarily the motivation it needed to mobilise excitement and political energy into a new project; to keep the free world safe from terrorism. However, things were going to be different this time.

Getting embroiled first in Afghanistan and later in Iraq placed a massive burden on the US economy, especially when embarking on unrealistic nation-building projects in their occupied countries. Soon the public back home became even more tired of these foreign wars of intervention. And after 20 years of occupation and a failed attempt at nation-building, the USA left Afghanistan in disgrace, having nothing to show for their efforts other than embarrassment.

However, the USA is now facing falling birth rates, social unrest and fragmentation. Despite their vast economic resources, they are declining faster and harder than any western power relative to their former position. Much of this is due to a failure to integrate disparate ethnic groups into a typical American cultural identity. A lot of Political focus and energy is spent on identity politics and infighting, leaving many uncertain about the future. This uncertainty dampens the excitement about settling down and having children. On top of this, the USA is also facing, like every other developed nation, falling birth rates due to individualism, higher education among a growing percentage of the population and careerism. These internal divisions in US politics are also spreading to the rest of the developed world, causing further political discord in European countries.

All these examples taken from Europe, Japan and USA illustrate the overarching tendency that developed countries that belong to the western world, or who are western adjacent in the case of Japan, are facing dwindling birth rates, exhaustion and an existential crisis.

Western European birth rate 1950-2021 (children per family)

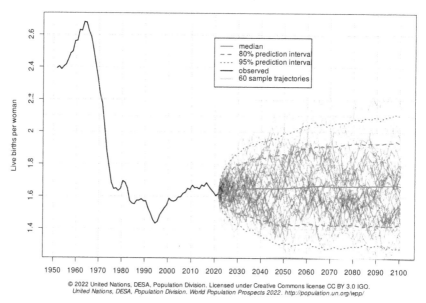

Ill. 4: Western European birth rate 1950-2021[16]

Explanation: These charts are from the Bayesian Hierarchical Modeling of total fertility that has been carried out with fertility estimates. Please note that only a small selection of the probabilistic trajectories of total fertility is displayed (gray lines) for illustration. The median projection is the solid bold red line, and the 80% and 95% projection intervals are displayed as dashed and dotted red lines respectively. At the country level, the high-low fertility variants correspond to +/- 0.5 child around the median trajectory displayed as blue dashed lines. The replacement-level of 2.1 children per woman is plotted as green horizontal dashed line only for reference.

---

[16] World Population Prospects. United Nations. [https://population.un.org/wpp/ Graphs/Probabilistic/FERT/TOT/926] (Accessed 19.10.22)

Eastern European birth rate 1950-2021 (children per family)

Eastern Europe

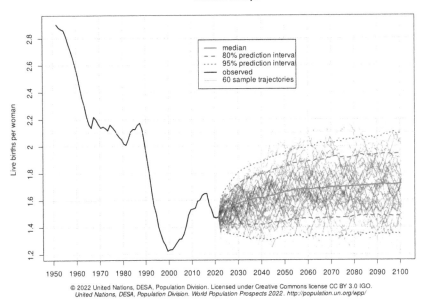

Ill. 5: Eastern European birth rate 1950-2021[17]

---

[17] World Population Prospects. United Nations. [https://population.un.org/wpp/ Graphs/Probabilistic/FERT/TOT/926] (Accessed 19.10.22)

Northern Europe population, mid-2020

In millions

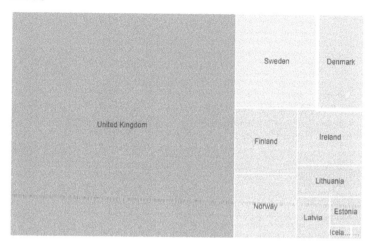

Total Fertility Rate

Lifetime births per woman

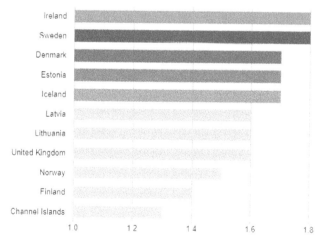

Ill. 6: Northern Europe population, mid-2020[18]

[18] Population Reference Bureau [https://interactives.prb.org/2020-wpds/europe/] (Accessed 27.07.22)

4. Why isn't the low birth rate discussed?

There are many reasons why low birth rates aren't discussed. Here are some of the most important reasons:

Birth rates are a long-term concern

Modern Europe has a short-term horizon. It sees problems of population growth as too far away to be of immediate concern. In addition, low birth rates take too long to become evident.

In the West, things have to happen this quarter, otherwise, there is no interest, and people focus on something else. The corporate mentality is reflected in quarterly reports. The managing director has to show immediate results or get kicked out. The 4-year term limit aggravates this that electoral politics is confined to, giving politicians little to no incentive to think or plan. These periods are insufficient when dealing with long-term demographic development that takes at least a generation before any noticeable effect can be observed.

No long-term guidelines

In past times, the birth rate was regulated by religion. European and Japanese societies have deregulated the religious mechanisms that have "coached" the birth rate. When European society became secularised, all perspectives on long-term birth rates slowly disappeared from the culture.

And the newly liberal political order that replaced the traditional order didn't care about family and birthrates in the same manner, placing individual liberation at the centre of its ideology and above that of the group.

One of the reasons why religion and tradition historically have been so successful as an ordering principle for society is because it encourages family structures conducive to birth rates above replacement level. If there had been a political solution that addressed the birth rate issue instead of religion, then there would have been historical evidence showing that high birth rates exist due to political decisions.

There are, of course, a few exceptions when countries increase their birth rates. Sweden did so from 1983-1987 but did not sustain the increase over the long term because, as always, some short-term thinking politicians used the country's future resources to win short-term political victories.

Still, Europe has no powerful demographic institutions to cope with the depopulation problem. If there had been political interest, a solid political or economic institution similar to the National Bank or the Central Bank would have emerged to take responsibility for the long-term birth rate, for example, a European birth rate Council. Such an institution, however, would also need strong protection to keep short-term thinking politicians from influencing it.

The "liberation" process.

Any person discussing the low birth rate problem will eventually come under fire from short-term thinkers for being too "conservative".

Because the birth rate problem is very complex, the effects of European depopulation have not been obvious until recently. Only now do we see signs that Europe and Japan are living off their parents' work. It is, of course, not economically or culturally self-sustainable.

During European society's "liberation" process, no political decisions were directed at solving the long-term problem of low birth rates. Some financial support was given, but the families' philosophical support and social prestige were just not there. The family, the basic unit of society, was regarded as boring, an idea popularised in practically all Western film- and entertainment industries. In the modern western world, no dedicated political institution morally supports a woman's decision to have children.

Support for women who want to bear children has been especially lacking at universities. Instead of having children early, female students wait until after their education is finished and they are well ahead in their careers. For women and men in Europe, this is like running on a "hamster-wheel". The fewer children you have, the longer you can fight and establish your career and, therefore, the longer you wait to have children. This development has been aggravating the problem of low birth rates. This mechanism also leads to especially low fertility among the segment of the population with the highest intellectual capacity, reducing their chances of passing their genes onto the next generation.

Journalistic self-censorship

"Oh, these things are touchy, touchy, touchy" one journalist said to me in an interview. "I would rather write about something else."

The population problem is a subject treated with extraordinary caution among Western journalists. The most important thing for a journalist is to be "politically correct" and not to step on anyone's toes. It is effortless to be labelled as a far-right "extreme" or something else equally derogatory if you write about this issue in a meaningful way. Also, as mentioned earlier, sustaining the right birth rate is a long-term problem that will not produce flashy headlines or clickbait. A low birth rate means nothing to journalists or editors concerned with the next day's front page. Questions of depopulation of Europeans in Europe are not sexy enough to make the first page, or even worse, directly foul tasting. So why bother?

And who would like to read about being faced with the possibility of giving up the "good and easy life"?

The result is self-censorship within the press. And this hurts society in the long run.

Yet because politicians are not taking responsibility for the problem, journalists should take the initiative and persuade politicians and the rest of society to look for concrete solutions. As we see, this is not the case.

5. The Great Replacement

Replacement Migration

The concept of The Great Replacement comes from France, and is first introduced and used by the author Camus in his book Le Grand Remplacement, where he argues that an european elite is in the process of replacing the native european population with people of immigrant origins.

Intertwined with the falling birth rates in Europe and other developed countries is the issue of replacement migration. Instead of encouraging its own native population to have enough children, politicians and policymakers are advocating for immigration[19] to replace the deficit of young working-age people. The result of this policy is the gradual replacement of the native European population with peoples of foreign origin, not considering heritage and cultural conditions. However, stating the obvious and pointing this out is met with condemnations of "racism" by bad faith actors, making the public debate near impossible.

Since the first version of this book was published in 2002, a more sinister turn of events has taken place in the public discourse around demographics. When the replacement of Europeans is described by liberal and progressive voices it is portrayed as something positive; it is welcomed by the press and politicians. However, when those who point out the negative sides of this replacement and want it to be stopped or reversed, it is

---

[19] United Nations. Department of Economic and Social Affairs.Population Division. Replacement Migration: Is it a Solution to Declining and Ageing Populations? vol. no. 206., United Nations, New York, 2001:

"... the report considers replacement migration for eight low-fertility countries (France, Germany, Italy, Japan, Republic of Korea, Russian Federation, United Kingdom and United States) and two regions (Europe and the European Union). Replacement migration refers to the international migration that a country would need to offset population decline and population ageing resulting from low fertility and mortality rates."
[https://www.un.org/en/development/desa/population/publications/ageing/replacement-migration.asp] (Accessed 11.07.22)

labelled as a "conspiracy theory" and denied by the very same press and politicians who previously lauded it.

In the following, you will see examples illustrating this.

Celebrated by the left

Media coverage of the changing demographics in the West is reported accurately when the reporter is positive about the change. Here are some examples:

Already on the 3. of Sep 2000, The Guardian wrote: "The last days of a white world" "We are near a global watershed – a time when white people will not be in the majority in the developed world, Britain included" and stating in the same article "[...] put a positive spin on the end of the white majority: 'If there are no majorities, then there are no minorities.' "[20].

Since then, this position has been increasingly more common in Western political commentary.

On the 21. of August 2012, The Business Insider published an article from The Economist that made the case that "Sweden Will Have To Become A Lot Less Blond"[21]. In the article, they write that:

"Sentiment towards immigrants is less negative than in many European countries.

As in many other countries, immigration is a divisive political issue in Sweden. This was reinforced by the entry into parliament of the immigration-critical Sweden Democrats (SD) in 2010. Public opinion on immigration is divided but appears to have been improving over the past 20 years."

[20] Browne, Anthony. 2000. The last days of a white world. Guardian News & Media Limited. [https://www.theguardian.com/uk/2000/sep/03/race.world] (Accessed 11.07.22)

[21] The Economist. 2012. Sweden Will Have To Become A Lot Less Blond. [https://www.businessinsider.com/sweden-politics-immigration-and-population-ageing-present-policy-challeng-2012-8?IR=T] (Accessed 11.07.22)

The New Republic wrote in an article in 2014: "Five Charts That Show Why a Post-White America Is Already Here If you're under 18, the future is now"[22].

US Census pointed out the same year (2014) in a headline that: "Projecting Majority-Minority – Non-Hispanic Whites May No Longer Comprise Over 50 Percent of the U.S. Population by 2044"[23].

National Public Radio reported in 2016 that: "Babies Of Color Are Now The Majority, Census Says". "Today's generation of schoolchildren looks much different than one just a few decades ago. Nonwhites are expected to become the majority of the nation's children by 2020, as our colleague Bill Chappell reported last year. This is now the reality among the very youngest Americans: babies"[24].

The Independent explained in 2016 the electoral victory of Trump with the ethnic anxiety of white Americans' fear of being replaced due to the rapid changes: "Donald Trump's greatest weapon is white Americans' fear that they're quickly becoming a minority – because they are". "In 1950 when Trump was four years old, the United States was 87.5 per cent non-Hispanic white, 10 per cent black and only 2.1 per cent Hispanic. By 2010, when Trump turned 64, the United States had become only 63.7 per cent non-Hispanic white, 16.3 per cent Hispanic and 12.3 per cent black. No other developed state has ever undergone ethnic change so rapid"[25].

[22] Frey, William H. 2014. Five Charts That Show Why a Post-White America Is Already Here. The New Republic [https://newrepublic.com/article/120370/five-graphics-show-why-post-white-america-already-here] (Accessed 11.07.22)

[23] U.S. Department of Commerce. 2014. Projecting Majority-Minority – Non-Hispanic Whites May No Longer Comprise Over 50 Percent of the U.S. Population by 2044 [https://www.census.gov/content/dam/Census/newsroom/releases/2015/cb15-tps16_graphic.pdf] (Accessed 11.07.22)

[24] Yoshinaga, Kendra. 2016. Babies Of Color Are Now The Majority, Census Says. npr. [https://www.npr.org/sections/ed/2016/07/01/484325664/babies-of-color-are-now-the-majority-census-says?t=1657549204009] (Accessed 11.07.22)

[25] Judah, Ben. 2016. Donald Trump's greatest weapon is white Americans' fear that they're quickly becoming... The Independent. [https://www.independent.co.uk/voices/donald-trump-us-elections-hillary-clinton-race-hispanic-black-vote-white-americans-fear-minority-true-a7402296.html] (Accessed 11.07.22)

Atlanta Black Star wrote the next year (2017): "The End of America's White Majority Is Near: What are the Implications?"[26]

In this article, they report that:

"The Census Bureau reported that in 2011 a majority of babies under age one, born in the United States, were non-white. A majority of American children will be Black or Brown by 2020, which is already the case in the U.S. K-12 public school system. Some institutions of higher learning, such as Harvard University, have responded to the new reality by admitting its first majority nonwhite first-year class."

In other words, the response to the demographic decline of white Americans is for an elite institution such as Harward to make a racially exclusively nonwhite first-year class. However, this is the opposite argument made. At the same time, there still was a white majority in the USA, when institutions were obliged to include quotas of etnic minorities into white majority classes. The argument is that because nonwhite minorities are minorities, we need to take extra care to include them. However, no such protection or special treatment seems to be afforded to the white part of the population now that they are becoming a minority. Now that nonwhite ethnic groups no longer have the prospect of remaining a minority, the argument changes to the exclusivity for those who are nonwhite, not including the future white minority.

Why is this the case? Where does this bias come from?

Further, we can read in the Brookings Institute celebrated this trend in 2018 in its article: "The US will become 'minority white' in 2045, Census projects – Youthful minorities are the engine of future growth"[28]

Washington Post had an article in 2018 that stated: "In a country where whites will lose majority status in about a quarter-century, and where research suggests that demographic anxiety is contributing to many of the social fissures polarising the United States, from immigration policy to

---

[26] Love, David. 2017. The End of America's White Majority Is Near: What are the Implications? Atlanta Black Star. [https://atlantablackstar.com/2017/09/12/end-americas-white-majority-near-implications/] (Accessed 11.07.22)

welfare reform to the election of President Trump, the story of the coming decades will be, to some degree, the story of how white people adapt to a changing country"[27].

Brookings Institute reported in 2019 that: "Less than half of US children under 15 are white, the census shows"[28].

The Chicago Reporter (2019): "The US white majority will soon disappear forever" stating that "By 2050, the US will be a 'majority-minority' country, with white non-Hispanics making up less than half of the total population."[29]

The new US president Joe Biden, when he was vice-president during the Obama administration, said the following[30]:

"Not only our Muslim communities but African communities, Asian communities, Hispanic communities and the wave continues. It's not going to stop. Nor should we want it to stop. It's one of the things I think we can be most proud of. [..] So there's a second thing in that bright box. An unrelenting stream of immigration. Non-stop. Folks like me, who are caucasian of European descent, for the first time in 2017, will be in an absolute minority in the United States of America. From then on, fewer than 50% of the people in America will be white European stock. That's not a bad thing. That's a source of our strength."

[27] McCoy, Terrence. 2018. White, and in the minority. The Washington Post. [https://www.washingtonpost.com/news/local/wp/2018/07/30/feature/majority-minority-white-workers-at-this-pennsylvania-chicken-plant-now-struggle-to-fit-in/] (Accessed 11.07.22)

[28] Frey, William H. 2019. Less than half of US children under 15 are white, census shows. The Brookings Institution. [https://www.brookings.edu/research/less-than-half-of-us-children-under-15-are-white-census-shows/] (Accessed 11.07.22)

[29] Poston, Dudley and Sáenz, Rogelio. 2019. The US white majority will soon disappear forever. The Chicago Reporter. [https://www.chicagoreporter.com/the-us-white-majority-will-soon-disappear-forever/] (Accessed 11.07.22)

[30] Gateway Pundit. 2018 Joe Biden: " Whites will be an ABSOLUTE minority in America - that's a source of our strength." Youtube. [https://www.youtube.com/watch?v=UgrliuQW_-Q] (Accessed 11.07.22)

As time passes, we can notice a change in the rhetoric from the established press and the Left, from the early 2000s and up until the 2020s. It goes from sober descriptive terms to a more and more positive framing and celebratory language. It is an excellent question, perhaps a forbidden question, to ask why this is.

Warnings from the right

A poll conducted by Harris Interactive in France on behalf of the new paper, Challenges[31], shows that 67 per cent of those participating in the poll were worried that there is a population replacement going on in their country, whereas those of French and European origin were displaced and replaced by immigration from Africa and the Middle East. According to this poll, the worry is greatest on the right, but substantial numbers on the left also reported Le Figaro[32] 21st of October in 2021.

The 2022 French election was a vote on replacement immigration. It brought a new and "radical" voice to the surface in the person of presidential candidate Éric Zemmour, who argued that France and the French people could not accept this replacement migration. He maintains that France's French and European heritage has an innate value in and of itself and can only be cherished and maintained by an ethnically French population.

The Gatestone institute reported back in 2021[33] that the coming French election would be about immigration and pointed to the increased crime, violence and polarisation in the country. Especially they were pointing out

[31] de Menthon, Pierre-Henri. 2021. 67% des Français s'inquiètent d'un "grand remplacement" Challenges. [https://www.challenges.fr/france/67-des-francais-s-inquietent-d-un-grand-remplacement_785793] (Accessed 11.07.22)

[32] Le Figaro. 2021. 67% de Français inquiets par l'idée d'un "grand remplacement", selon un sondage. [https://www.lefigaro.fr/actualite-france/67-de-francais-inquiets-par-l-idee-d-un-grand-remplacement-selon-un-sondage-20211021] (Accessed 11.07.22)

[33] Meotti, Giulio. 2021. France to Vote on the Great Replacement of Western Civilization. The Gatestone institute. [https://www.gatestoneinstitute.org/17843/france-election-immigration] (Accessed 11.07.22)

the growth of the Muslim population in France. They further quoted the open letter that French military servicemen signed and sent to their president Macron:

"Two thousand military servicemen signed a letter to French President Emmanuel Macron and the government, warning that France is on the verge of collapse and the civil war because the state has "surrendered" to radical Muslims. The letter followed an appeal by 20 retired generals and hundreds of former officers, in which they speak of "disintegration and Islamization" in progress, as well as a document sent to parliament by other generals and officers, proclaiming, "We are in a hybrid war, it is multifaceted and will end in a civil war at best and a cruel defeat with no future at worst".

These are stark words coming from people whose calling in life was patriotic service to their country, placing their own lives on the line if need be.

However, such warnings and pointing out the same facts that many liberal institutions celebrate are brushed aside by authorities and the press; denounced as a "conspiracy theory". Often referring to "The Great Replacement" as one of the most dangerous conspiracy theories. One example is from an article in The Guardian (2022)[34], the same news outlet that in 2000 reported on this demographic trend in a positive framing. The Guardian news article from 2022 reports that an [...] 18-year-old alleged shooter is said to have endorsed the "great replacement theory". And then goes on to mention Fox News host Tucker Carlson and Hungarian president Viktor Orbán in the next two paragraphs as guilt by association:

"The Fox News host Tucker Carlson had mentioned replacement theories more than 400 times on his show before the shooting. Afterwards, he initially sought to distance himself from it. "We're still not sure exactly what it is," he claimed on his show on 17 May. In the next breath, though, he doubled down. "Here's what we do know, for a fact: there's a strong

---

[34] Rose, Steve. 2022. A deadly ideology: how the 'great replacement theory' went mainstream. [https://www.theguardian.com/world/2022/jun/08/a-deadly-ideology-how-the-great-replacement-theory-went-mainstream] (Accessed 11.08.22)

political component to the Democratic party's immigration theory … and they say out loud: 'We are doing this because it helps us to win elections.'"

Two days after the shooting in Hungary, the newly re-elected prime minister, Viktor Orbán, was also doubling down. In a televised speech to mark the start of his fourth term, he claimed he was fighting against "the great European population exchange … a suicidal attempt to replace the lack of European, Christian children with adults from other civilisations – migrants"."

The premise for what is called "The Great Replacement" conspiracy theory by liberal establishment institutions in the West is that this demographic trend is intentional and promoted by authorities and institutions across the western world. It is very curious, then, that as long as this demographic development is portrayed positively, it is welcomed to speak about it by these same institutions and newspapers, and it is not denied or denounced.

However, even if this demographic change is not promoted with an intention on the part of our liberal institutions and authorities here in the West, the responsibility still lies with our governing bodies, who have the power to act and can stop this demographic development. At the very least, they are guilty of gross negligence.

Who steers the political agenda?

Power always gravitates into the hands of the organised few who are capable of a modicum of collective action for the sake of their common class, religious or group interest. And in our globalised age there is an increasingly centralised financial and transnational elite that governs the movements of the world.

This transnational elite consists of about 2153 billionaires according to the Time magazine in January 2020[35]. At the forefront of this global elite are the ultra rich and influential families, such as; the Rotschilds, Rockefellers, Morgans, Du Pont, Bush, Clintons, The Ford Foundation and Soros to mention the most known among them. As a result the high impact levers of control over the financial system that dominates our world, as well as ownership over the press and mass media, has ended up in the hands of very few people. This power rests on direct and indirect ownership, and the control of credit and capital flows. Nation states can be brought to their knees without access to the international capital markets, and most nations in the world have huge government debt; some of it larger than can ever be paid off. All of this is made possible through the practice of fractional reserve banking; propagated through an international central bank system. In addition to this, the biggest companies in the world are Vanguard, Blackrock and State Street Corporation, between them are the biggest shareholders in Apple, Facebook, Lockheed Martin, Tesla, MasterCard, Dupont, General Electric, Fox, Disney, Microsoft, Paramount and IBM[36]. A key to maintaining this control is to keep their power, ownership and methods of control opaque and out of the public limelight. As long as this stays out of the public mind there will be no meaningful opposition to it, and their power is safe.

This global elite wants to direct and manipulate elections worldwide by funding activist groups, NGOs and big media companies, including social media companies. Mass immigration of millions of people into the west also plays a big part in this. Massive migration across borders causes social fragmentation and as a result the bonds of national loyalty and common identity are broken down. When social trust and cohesion disintegrates, due to a lack of common customs, heritage and identity, societies become less resistant to outside manipulation. New immigrants do not usually share the

---

[35] 2020. Bates, Josiah. Billionaires Have More Wealth Than 60% of the World's Population, Report Finds. TIME USA, LLC. [https://time.com/5768346/billionaires-wealth/] (Accessed 11.08.22)

[36] Reuters Fact Check. 2022. [https://www.reuters.com/article/factcheck-business-investment-idUSL2N2WI1K4] Reuters (Accessed 11.08.22)

same interests and degree of loyalty to the new nation that they now inhabit as compared to the native population. And being uprooted from their own previous nation many immigrants exist in a fluctuating rootless limbo, this creates a situation of vulnerability and dependency. This dependency can be turned into political power by actors who know how to play on this.

This allows for a new breed of globally oriented politicians that use these new immigrants as voting cattle, by offering them "protection" and free benefits in exchange for their votes. As a consequence these politicians rely less and less on votes from their own native populations, and thus are not obliged to win votes by promoting policies that have traditionally been regarded as common national interests. Furthermore, these globally oriented politicians are typically also the recipients of support and donations from the transnational financial class. This further divides and weakens western nations, making it more difficult for the native population of these nations to assert their national interests versus the international financial powers. This type of immigration is promoted by people such as billionaire and finance mogul George Soros through The Open Society Foundation, an NGO that he funds[37]. This is not unlike the divide and conquer strategy of former colonial powers, however in a much more subtle way. Thus the entire political system in the west is subverted away from serving the interest of its native population and skewed towards serving the interests of powerful transnational financial elites.

The primary object of this power structure is to keep its power. That is the iron rule of all power constellations that want to propagate itself and the benefits it confers on its beneficiaries. Only in this case the beneficiaries are not the peoples of a certain country

This transnational financial elite and their companies influence and manipulate liberal and leftist people that do not understand that they are pawns governed by the richest and most cynical capitalists in the world.

---

[37] 2017. Monroe, Nick. The Soros Saga. [https://medium.com/@nickmon1112/the-soros-saga-a487518e2869] (Accessed 11.08.22)

Vanguard, Blackrock and State Street Corporation own and control Big Pharma[38] and well known companies such as Pfizer, Moderna, Coca-Cola[39], Monsanto[40] and so on. Just to give an example, Pfizer had an advertisement budget of 21,11 Billion USD in the time periode 2009-2019[41] and sometimes pays the lion's share of the advertisement income of many papers, TV and radio stations. This kind of money gives power and influence.

But there is hope. The liberal press has slowly been losing its grip over the last two decades. CNN has lost 90% of the viewers[42]. Many papers have to close or radically cut down the employees. CNN+ had to close after 2 months while only having 10.000 subscribers despite a marketing budget of 400 million USD.

In the USA 59% of the people said they agree with the statement: That "most news organizations are more concerned with supporting an ideology

[38] 2021. Dr. Mercola, Joseph. Who Owns Big Pharma + Big Media? You'll Never Guess. Children's Health Defense. [https://childrenshealthdefense.org/defender/blackrock-vanguard-own-big-pharma-media/] (Accessed 11.08.22)

[39] 2022. YU., JEA. Top 4 Mutual Fund Holders of Coca-Cola. Dotdash Meredith. [https://www.investopedia.com/articles/investing/032116/top-4-mutual-fund-holders-cocacola-ko-vtsmx.asp] (Accessed 11.08.22)

[40] 2021. Sarich, Christina. Who are Really the Top Shareholders of Monsanto? Natural Society. [https://naturalsociety.com/who-are-really-the-top-shareholders-of-monsanto/] (Accessed 11.08.22)

[41] Pfizer's advertising spending in the United States from 2009 to 2019. Statista GmbH.
[https://www.statista.com/statistics/192112/us-ad-spending-of-pfizer/] (Accessed 11.08.22)

[42] 2022. Anderson, Natasha. Tuning out! Viewership at scandal-plagued CNN plummets by as much as 90% from last year in both overall audience and in advertiser-coveted 25-to-54 demographic. Associated Newspapers Ltd. [https://www.dailymail.co.uk/news/article-10394997/CNN-loses-nearly-90-advertiser-coveted-demographics-overall-total-audience.html] (Accessed 11.08.22)

or political position than with informing the public"[43]. People all over the world are waking up in droves to these facts, especially in the USA because this is where the battle of the future global order will be decided.

We see the BRICS countries are leaving the petrodollar and moving in towards a new gold and silver based system. On the 12th of March 2022 Russia linked its national currency, the ruble, to gold. The 19th of March Saudi Arabia's Crown Prince Muhammed Bin Salman and China's Xi Jin Ping agreed to decrease the influence of the petrodollar.

BRICS are also building their version of the SWIFT system, called SPFS. India's ATMs might soon be ready to take Russian Mir debit and credit cards[44].

This means that Vanguard, Blackrock and State Street Corp will lose trillions of dollars and a significant amount of control in these countries.

Hopefully many immigrants will want to go back to their own countries when industry and production in their countries of origin will begin to grow. It is reasonable to anticipate that there will be economic growth in these countries, once the debt based money system, and global companies such as Vanguard and Balckrock, will not hinder local small and middle-sized companies from growing into national and regional alternatives.

Have faith. Be free in your thoughts. Do your own research. We will win this information war!

[43] 2021. Meek, Andy. Fewer Americans Than Ever Before Trust The Mainstream Media. Forbes Media LLC
[https://www.forbes.com/sites/andymeek/2021/02/20/fewer-americans-than-ever-before-trust-the-mainstream-media/?sh=16cee3cd282a] (Accessed 11.08.22)

[44] Srivastava, Shruti and Beniwal, Vrishti. 2022. Russia offers SWIFT alternative to India for rouble payments. The Printers (Mysore) Private Ltd.
[https://www.deccanherald.com/business/business-news/russia-offers-swift-alternative-to-india-for-rouble-payments-1096109.html] (Accessed 4.10.22)

6. The current position of European culture

Below you will find the words of Professor Alexander Tytler, who in the eighteenth century studied and analysed democracies. His work tells us where European democracy is heading – or more precisely; falling apart:

"A democracy cannot exist as a permanent form of government. It can only exist until the voters discover that they can vote themselves money from the public treasury. From that moment on, the majority always votes for the candidates promising the most money from the public treasury, with the result that a democracy always collapses over loose fiscal policy, and is followed by a dictatorship."

Professor Alexander Tytler, 1778

Development stages	Estimated years
From bondage to spiritual faith	1500-1600
From spiritual faith to great courage	1600-1700
From courage to liberty	1700-1800
From liberty to abundance	1800-1900
From abundance to selfishness	1900-1950
From selfishness to complacency	1950-2000
From complacency to apathy	2000-2020
From apathy to dependency	*2020-2030
From dependency back to bondage	2030-2040

*Here we are now

Table 4: Professor Alexander Tytler, 1778[45]

---

[45] What If Alexander Tytler Was Right? - American Thinker. [https://www.americanthinker.com/articles/2021/03/what_if_alexander_tytler_was_right.html] (Accessed 24.10.22)

The average length in age of the world's great civilisations has been two hundred years. These nations have progressed through the following sequence: bondage to spiritual faith, spiritual faith to great courage, courage to liberty, liberty to abundance, abundance to selfishness, selfishness to complacency, complacency to apathy, apathy to dependence, dependency back to bondage.

From complacency to apathy.

This is where we are now,

and the terror attacks have just started.

There will be much, much more.

Professor Tytler's view is shared by many history professors, particularly in the United States. These professors' theories are often variations of Professor Tytler's staircase cycle of democracy. We use the Tytler staircase in our book because Tytler was one of the first western historians to employ such a graph. Other thinkers who share Tytler's principle view of democratic societies are Matthew Mielko, a professor of sociology, Arnold Toynbee, an English historian working in the middle of the twentieth century, Caroll Quigley, professor of history at Georgetown University, and William McNeill, professor of history at Chicago University.

These prominent professors and historians view history long-term and fight off all short-sighted views of our society. Unfortunately, such long-term thinking is not in charge of western societies.

7. The Western EGO - Thinking

What is going on in the Western brain?

According to the liberal view, everybody should make up their own brain/mind and create their own individual point of view. This contrasts with religious societies, where ideological settings are already fixed.

Freedom of choice creates a lot of uncertainty in people. Many people in the West feel alone or alienated from society and are willing to do whatever it takes to acquire the shelter of a dominant religion or a society with strict rules. Examples include Mr John Walker Lindh, the US citizen who fought for the Taliban, or Western women who converted to Islam. These people want clear rules. They want to know what is good and what is bad. They want someone to give them rules and directions. Others seek answers in authoritarian ideologies and political movements. These are some of the reactions to the political climate and psychological uncertainty that currently rules in the west.

Another reaction to this psychological uncertainty is to become even more atomised and self-absorbed. That orientates the modern Western self to think in a concise term. Short-term-oriented societies will die out within 50 years. It is one of the reasons why democracies have been few and have existed for short periods in history.

Short-sighted thoughts spin around in the Western brain: How can I make money? What can I buy? What's hot today? What's in fashion? Who's famous? Views, ideas, and directions change from month to month. In some media, views change weekly, or even throughout the day.

These two polar opposite reactions to the modern liberal order create tension in western societies. The ideologically fragile Westerners are tossed back and forth and don't know how to stay focused on long-term views.

The increasing speed of information is kicking people around, and only the mentally disciplined and well-educated can sort out the chaos of liberal ideas and hold a strict philosophy.

For a large portion of the Western population, there is an ironic duality; they seek novelties and praise all which is marketed as new and progressive, yet at the same time view real change as a threat; they do not want to adapt to the new situation we are in.

When "I" becomes more important than "we", the egocentric approach takes control and decreases the number of children born. The self-absorbed ego concentrates on amusements such as games, shopping, TV watching, clubbing, and so on. When thoughts about "I" start to block the mind, there are no thoughts about the future; or about how to make society and culture survive.

This is the reason why the Taliban destroyed all the TVs they found in Afghanistan. Maybe they do not even understand why they just had an instinctive feeling that TV is not good.

Yes, television and internet entertainment is disastrous for sex life as well. It redirects our attention from immediacy and intimacy with those close to us and acts as a cold and impersonal intermediator.

Everywhere in the Western world, whenever TV transmissions or the internet have been interrupted for a long time, many babies are conceived. At these moments, people saw reality and reacted to it.

"Netflix and chill" are ego trips

Why are so-called "Netflix and chill" so popular? Because they involve the ego. It is much easier to turn on the computer or control the button on the TV remote control than it is to face your real-life situation.

TV series and computer games simulate having a tribe to relate to and somebody to gossip around. You can discuss the characters with your best friends over the phone or chat with them on the Internet about what happened on the latest episode of your favourite TV show.

Short-term entertainment is easy to accept. You can keep all problems away. National cable and broadcasting, and the global internet, create a society where the masses watch TV and streaming and do not engage in real life. And thus can easily be directed by a liberal elite that doesn't watch TV themselves. The result of addiction to TV and internet entertainment is lower birth rates, ultimately meaning no future.

The sex drive in a natural and healthy environment is our future. Yes, the sex drive is often politically and sociologically incorrect, but it is still our future. And social isolation and stigmatisation of natural healthy sex drive in men due to mass hysteria driven by internet network effects, such as "me too," are discouraging healthy sexual development and pair bonding between the sexes.

Once adolescence and the first years as a young adult are over, a new burden is introduced on healthy fertile couples as they enter into careers and "working life"; people in the West have fewer children today because the demands put on parents are too great. It goes against the instinct of our species.

Humankind's instinct is to breed as much as possible. Still, Western society has established so many rules and laws concerning reproduction that people, especially men, do not want to have children. There are meagre incentives for the individual man to make these sacrifices when he gets so little in return, unlike in a more traditional society where he could expect to become respected as the head of a household. This is one of the major reasons why the West will fall and why fewer and fewer high-quality men are willing to commit to the long-term obligation of raising children. A more reasonable thing would be to have rules and institutions that worked in synergy with the instincts of our species, not going against them.

I am not promoting any Taliban-type measures, but I want to stimulate a discussion to persuade the press and our politicians to balance short-term views with long-term thinking.

Perhaps the Western world needs at least one TV-free evening per week. It would be interesting to see the results of one TV-free Friday or Saturday evening for one year. My optimistic prediction is that the birth rates will increase at least 50%.

During the most recent war in Afghanistan, an English woman journalist dressed up in a "burka" or "chador" (a veil covering a woman's face) so that nobody would recognise her as a Western woman. She met an Afghan woman telling her: "It does not matter how many of us you will kill. We, the Afghans, will have another ten children while you will have one or none." The English journalist was so astonished by this cultural perspective that her report became one of Afghanistan's most important articles.

After that, when Mr. bin Laden's plans to attack the World Trade Center were fulfilled on September 11th, 2001, an interesting reaction came. In the US, women started to become pregnant, and the isolated feeling of many people in the US went away. Americans needed each other again, and subconsciously they wanted to survive. This is a typical reaction. When society is threatened, people change their outlook from the short to the long term, which is also what happened In the US.

Mr. bin Laden took up a sleeping elephant that had gotten lethargic after the end of the cold war. Thanks to Mr. bin Laden, for a brief moment, it looked like there was energy to muster and hope for the Western world; but only if that is, we learned the lesson. This would also have given meaning to the deaths of the thousands of people who died in the attacks on the World Trade Center. But alas, as we have witnessed, it was not enough. It looks like something even more drastic and intense is needed to revitalise the western world and shake it from its slumber.

Changing your view from a short-term egoistic view to a long-term "we" view is the best guarantee for a future society with wholesome human values.

By only thinking of your career and how much money you can earn, you will only prove Mr. bin Laden right in what he thought about the West; decadent, morally weak and self-absorbed. His tribe and population are increasing. The West's population is dying. At this rate, it's just a matter of time, and Western culture will die if we do not change our ways.

Thus, not having children is the most egotistical choice you can make. You are consuming today's resources and leaving nothing for the future. People with a short-term view argue that there are many poor children worldwide. Let's take care of them.

This view is also very selfish. This mentality implies the Western view is the best world view. It means we know how to raise our children (if we have any) and that other cultures do not. When adopted children or immigrants come to the West, they bring their culture with them in one way or another. This culture that these immigrants bring with them is incompatible with our traditions and worldview; it has organically developed in our ecology, particularly our people, over thousands of years. The effect of this is alienation, social fragmentation and democratic collapse.

We already see the first outbursts of wishful thinking that says we can bring all other children and immigrants to the West and that these children will adapt to Western egocentric values. Of course, they won't because their long-term view will be superior to the short-term views of Western pundits and talking heads. By not having children, you forget everything your ancestors did. What they did for you to be here.

A modern person has to think about so many things. Due to technology, life might be physically less challenging now than a hundred years ago or more, but the psychological stress and mental demands are more intense than ever. If you want to make it big in the modern world, you're locked into the "rat race"; career, work and education, leaving little time and energy for family life and procreation.

No wonder the Westerner wants to escape all these demands and turns to the TV or computer. In these interactions, you can "turn off your brain" and watch other people being told what to do. However, by turning off the TV, you get the opportunity to gain new self-respect.

You are forcing your neighbour's children to work harder to preserve our society by not having children. When you live a selfish life, you leave the few kids in the next generation to take care of the whole burden. And there is no guarantee that they will be able to shoulder this burden, let alone have the incentives to do so.

One projection from Pew Research Center shows that the Muslim population in Europe can almost triple from 4,9% (in 2016) to 14% in 2050[46]. How do you think this will impact the future of Europe and the world at large? What will this entail for the future of ethnic European children? When looking to history as a guide, it is a fair assumption to say that this will invite conflict and perhaps the downfall of our nations as we know them. What we hold to be dear and true will not have a future in this demographic development. We must take action now.

Many people react to such information by saying, "Oh, by that time, you will be dead and buried."

But hey, what about your children, or if you do not have any, your relatives' or your friend's children? Are we going to hand over an outrageous world to the next generation without feeling ashamed? There is a certain callousness to not care about the future of your kin. It is to place oneself outside the life cycle, the ultimate spiritual and biological death.

The Western egocentric process can be traced to Immanuel Kant, Kaliningrad (Konigsberg). Kant developed the concept of modern Western identity and encouraged people to think of the inner, isolated self. Egoism comes from the Latin word ego, which equals "I".

Kant developed the concept of egoism in his anthropological work beginning in 1798. (See more in the Chapter "Philosophical approach") When Louis Descartes, the French Philosopher that died in 1654 in Stockholm, announced "cogito ergo sum" — "I think, therefore I exist," it marked the beginning of egocentric thinking in Western society. And Immanuel Kant built upon this and spread it to all of modern European thinking.

It was also the beginning of the modern concept of art in the Western Hemisphere: the artistic genius, a painter or sculptor, for example, who is at the forefront of cultural thought. But the artistic genius is only focused on themself and the trip to the inner self. This egocentricity has become

---

[46] 5 facts about the Muslim population in Europe. Pew Research Center. [https://www.pewresearch.org/fact-tank/2017/11/29/5-facts-about-the-muslim-population-in-europe/] (Accessed 11.07.22)

ingrained in society since Descartes' time. For a long time, the Church, with its conservative grip, managed to resist, but because Western church leaders are also directed by egocentricity, society only really moved in one direction.

Communism was a philosophical attempt to balance the progress of liberal egocentricity, but communism could only fail. Communism turned out to be the worst idol worshipping in the world -the cult of Stalin and Mao.

Under liberalisation, the ego becomes more important in the West. Faith disappears and is replaced by your focus on yourself. Rock stars and movie stars replace God and saints. And when faith fades away, society becomes very fragile.

At the same time, other parts of the world have kept their old religious system. By keeping their faith, these societies have seen their populations increase tremendously. They will never accept Western liberal values because they know instinctively that the Western world is dying because of this modern paradigm.

Muslims and East Asian cultures, excluding Japan occupied by the US after WW2, feel assured that they will survive. They have solid cultural confidence and healthy birth rates.

Like what the Taliban woman said to a Western woman reporter when the journalists entered Afghanistan after the attacks on the 11thof September 2001:

"You may kill some of our sons, but we will give birth to 10 more, while you won't give birth to anyone."

Can the statement be clearer?

At the same time, an overflow of information is flooding us daily, distracting us.

What can you believe? How can you sort this information overload? Faith and tradition is the system that you use to filter information. Without a tradition to support yourself, the Western person is fragile and alone and thus an easy target for manipulation and subversion from those who want to gain an advantage.

The old established press focus is turning increasingly toward the promotion of egocentricity. Newspapers and magazines are becoming more focused on the individual. The lion's share of articles is dedicated to individual personal matters. What the future will bring is an unpopular subject because that information is very distressing to most people; consequences require hard decisions and efforts on our part.

All evidence points to the fact that liberal democracy doesn't have the tools to cope with these long-term challenges. This is by no means remedied by the established press that selectively focuses on the ego programs of famous politicians.

Analytical publications die out because they cannot compete with the tempo of ego-focused tabloids and the clickbait mentality promoted by many newspapers.

Faith and tradition also disappear when people think only of the short-term and are replaced with the worship of rock stars and actors. How many love songs are about family values and fertility? None, of course.

At the same time, the Internet is also increasing the fixation on sex and porn. Especially giving young men an illusory and brief satisfaction by diverting their sexual drive away from productive activities, eventually leaving them more empty and depressed than before. And no woman has become pregnant through an Internet cable.

What can change the course of self-destruction that Europe and the other developed countries are on? You need a powerful young rebel to destroy the well-constructed house this old ego-focused generation has built.

This young rebel must have strong natural charisma and a deep personal conviction in their cause. Such a young rebel must be larger than life and able to captivate the imagination of a generation and fuel it with excitement. We need a youth rebellion. A daring movement of virility and pro vitality. They fearlessly can express themselves in art, music, literature and family life.

The problem is that today's youth hasn't learned how to rebel. The parents of today's youth caught the cud of liberal movements in the sixties. Still, these same parents dedicated themselves to making money and didn't bother to teach their children about youth movements. These parents do not want to spend time teaching their children about their pasts, so today's youth lack organisation and the courage needed to make a change.

Those who are a little older and have more resources and experience should encourage and support young, charismatic youth leaders and help them organise, but never tell them what to do or say. It must be a genuine expression coming from that generation, and they must also have the freedom to gain their own experiences.

8. Educated people have fewer children

There is an urgent need to change how government support is distributed. All over the world, the number of children with educated parents is declining. The more educated the parents, the fewer children they have. It should be the other way around. If you are smart, you should have children to pass your genes on.

The current trend is that uneducated people tend to have more children than educated ones. If we analyse history, we will find that modern and complex societies demand a certain level of skills and knowledge to function. As soon as this level falls, liberal democracy will become even more dysfunctional.

If this idea is true, we are expecting the demise of democracy, more extensive wars, more organised crime, more organised terrorism, and the disintegration of our nations. It is of utmost importance that governments encourage women with higher education to have many children.

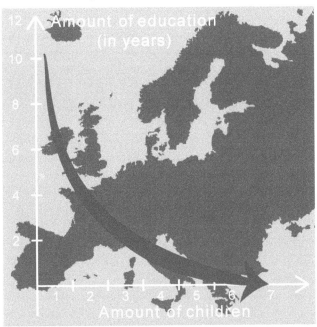

Ill. 6: Amount of education and children

We also strongly need governments to support women who are employed or are going through education and already have many children. Support may include daycare and night care centres, housekeeping services, and the opportunity to resume a career.

Politicians have to be strong and stand up for these policies because there will be critics saying that this support is not fair. Our future depends on intelligent and educated women having children. It is a question of life or death for our society.

The European world and politicians must understand basic demographics like corporate directors must care for their companies. Imagine Tesla's corporate leadership not supporting the Tesla brand and product. What would It mean for the corporation's future? Surely it would sooner or later go out of business.

We must acknowledge that the West's population is significant to keeping our tradition of freedom and liberty alive and promoting scientific research and development progress.

When there are 9-12 billion people in the world, simple statistics show that even more, progressive organisations will want to reshape the world in their twisted image and, as a result, destroy the world in the process. Rich egocentric intellectuals will lead these organisations. The World Economic Forum, headed by Klaus Schwab, is an excellent example.

Many cultures survive by not educating their women, promoting them towards early marriage and motherhood, and encouraging a domestic lifestyle. Educated women have fewer children than uneducated women, as we have seen. Therefore following this logic, cultures with many educated women will, over time, die out. If nothing is done to remedy this.

The influence of modern Western culture, which includes women's education, will be strongly resisted by many countries. Such as Afghanistan. Despite 20 years of US occupation and billions of US dollars spent on attempts at liberal education and reforming the Afghan population, they did not get any closer to their goal of transforming Afghanistan, or Afghan women, into modern liberals.

Leaders in these countries know that educating women would destroy the entire order and thus the future of their people and culture. Some countries have decided to resist and fight the West, with force if necessary. Because they view the global liberal order, which is dominated by the West, as an existential threat.

The West can still use its technological and organisational skills to dominate for a while. In the long run, Western culture will lose since it does not have a large enough quantity compared to quality. Within 50 years, the West's share of the world's population will drop from today's 15% down to 5%. Therefore the culture that is able to combine both quality and quantity will be the winner.

Which cultures will survive then? And who will become the new dominant force?

Not the European world, given the shape it is in today. And not Japan either, judging by the current situation. Too many sclerotic and rigid organisations in these countries oppose necessary change and revitalisation. There are no signs that a significant birth rate increase in Europe or the Anglo-Saxon sphere will occur anytime soon.

Some other cultures will take over and dominate the world. The likely candidates are China or India. And right now, it looks like China is winning out. China has had the strongest growth in GDP in the world and is rapidly catching up to the USA. However, we cannot count other countries out.

India can become the leading culture in the future, combining a large number of scientists and a history of the institutional rule of law, as well as being fluent in English.

India also has the fundamentals of a fertile population – providing the right number of people needed to support the future society. Also, some of the religions in India are very supportive of women bearing children and have also been considerably open to women's education at the same time.

Russia has the possibility to be one of the major players in the world on the condition that its economy will improve enough to support a birth rate increase. Historically, the Russians have been able to increase their population when necessary.

This question will be determined by the skills of the Russian leadership, since changes in Russia come from the top down, just like in India. Russia has a large number of highly-educated women who could easily have many children if supported in the right way.

All of these countries are also members of what is known as BRICS. BRICS is a collection of the world's leading emerging economies, and the member countries are as follows: Brasil, Russia, India, China and South Africa. This is an international coalition to cooperate and promote their own self-interests vis a vis the current western US lead global domination. The de facto purpose of BRICS is to create a multipolar world where all these countries are free to pursue their path and destiny.

Tax System

One way to remedy the current demographic situation is to use the tax system. The Soviet Union imposed a personal tax on those individuals who did not have any children. The tax amounted to 6% of personal income and provided a strong enough incentive to change the demographic development. We can easily see how economic factors influence the decision to have children.

In today's democracy, this might be difficult because there are more and more households consisting of only one person. Politicians smart enough to support a society that balances quality and quantity will face voters who will say: "No. I do not want to support families. I want to live by myself and support myself. Therefore, I vote for party X."

This is a question of democracy in the short run vs the long term. It is one of the shortcomings of today's democracy. Democracy cannot survive in the long term when it is geared only towards the short term.

Information is important. If enough people in Europe could be convinced that their liberties are at stake and to hang on to these personal liberties, they would have to pay the extra 6% of a no-children tax or have children themselves, and then maybe the European mindset would change. Here I am going to say something optimistic: Western youth have a very developed capacity for empathy, and if they believe the course is right, they are willing to sacrifice.

Together with tax reform, there should be an avalanche of information explaining why the extra tax is introduced and what they will get in return. And that the goal should be to have children of your own, a source of meaning, purpose and happiness.

Taxes need to be transferred from singles to couples with children. Iceland and Luxemburg are heroes *(from 1st ed. numbers, 1998)*.

Russia had lost a lot of people since the removal of the No-children tax after the liberation from communism. Before, every person in the Soviet Union had to pay 12% tax if they had no children.

When that tax was removed the birth rate fell from 2.4 to 1.1 children per woman per lifetime. I bring this example up to show that government policies and incentives do have an effect on the birth rates and the demographic development in a country.

During my time at the Delovoy Peterburg, a daily industry newspaper in Russia, we arranged seminars and published articles and advertisements in order to increase the fertility rate in the country. During this time I wrote the book Old Europe Shame on You in Russian and in English and sent 1200 copies to the EU members of Parliament and 600 copies to the Russian Duma. And I encourage others to get involved and to do similar efforts.

Income tax compared from 2021

Country	Single	Couple	Diff.
Switzerland	22.80	10.64	12.16
Poland	34.85	14.27	20.58
Ireland	33.96	19.00	14.96
Luxembourg	40.21	19.66	20.54
Iceland	32.15	20.02	12.13
Czech Republic	39.91	21.81	18.11
Lithuania	37.60	23.59	14.01
Denmark	35.43	25.70	9.73
United Kingdom	31.25	26.98	4.27
Estonia	38.05	28.91	9.14
Netherlands	35.33	29.07	6.26
Slovenia	43.61	29.46	14.15
Slovak Republic	41.33	29.59	11.74
Hungary	43.16	30.51	12.65
Portugal	41.84	30.88	10.96
Latvia	40.53	31.37	9.16
Norway	35.96	32.56	3.39
Germany	48.09	32.75	15.35
Greece	36.70	33.15	3.54
Spain	39.25	33.83	5.43
Austria	47.82	34.14	13.68
Belgium	52.62	37.29	15.33
Sweden	42.57	37.56	5.01
Italy	46.52	37.90	8.62
Finland	42.71	38.57	4.14
France	47.01	39.01	8.00

Table 5: Income tax compared from 2021[47]

Note: Tax difference single person at 100% average earnings without child; and one-earner married couple at 100% average earnings, with two children.

---

[47] Taxing Wages - Comparative Tables. [https://stats.oecd.org/Index.aspx?DataSetCode=AWCOMP] (Accessed 19.10.22)

Demographic Heroes

Iceland and Luxembourg are the demographic heroes of Europe. They show that it is possible to have a birth rate over 2.1 when the transfer tax is in effect. The transfer tax sends money from singles to people with children. The Czech Republic is also admirable for its transfer tax program, yet for now, the birth rate in the Czech Republic is well below 2.1 (The fertility rate is relatively low at 1.64 births per woman in 2020).

Having many children should be profitable. If the owner of a forest cuts down his trees, he is forced by the law to replant new trees. If a European person chooses to concentrate only on him/herself, such a person is in effect cutting down a tree. But there is no law telling him or her to replant. We will have devastated countries in Europe.

Therefore, the information campaign has to include an explanation of how the transfer tax supports the future of the country and how it will guarantee personal freedoms in the long run, not only for you living now but also for coming generations.

The information campaign can be combined with an information campaign for pensions. In the Scandinavian countries, the pension system was designed to be supported by future generations. These generations are not being regenerated. Within the coming decade, the pension system in Sweden will collapse.

The success of Hungary

Hungary is one of the European countries in recent history that managed to turn the trend of this demographic development around. When Viktor Orbán became Hungary's prime minister in 2010, birth rates were well below replacement rates. The new government in Hungary took active measures to become a "family-friendly country". They promote "family policy" and distinguish it from "social policy". Family policy is regarded as an investment in the country's future and is not considered an expense or a financial burden. Hungary spends about 5% of their GDP on pro-family policies. Now about ten years later, we can see the benefits paying off. The birth rate is up 20% from 2010 and growing[48].

Family Affairs Minister in Hungary, Katalin Novák, stated that the Hungarian government wants to put young couples in a position to have as many children as they want and to support an environment for couples to have children free of any financial difficulties.

To this end, Viktor Orban and the Hungarian government have proposed a seven-point plan[49], stating that "this – not immigration – is the response of the Hungarian people":

1. He said that the Government would introduce an allowance for young married couples aimed at encouraging them to have children. Every woman under the age of forty who gets married for the first time will be eligible for a preferential loan of up to HUF 10 million. Repayment of the loan will be suspended for three years after the birth of a child and for another three years after a second. In addition, one-third of the loan's principal will be written off after the birth of a second child. If a third child is born, the remaining debt will be cancelled in its entirety.

2. Preferential loans available under the already established family housing benefit scheme will be extended. At present, families with two children can receive low-interest loans of HUF 10 million for the purchase of new homes, while families with three or more children have access to preferential loans of HUF 15 million. In the future, families with two or more children will also be able to use such loans for the purchase of existing properties.

3. Up until now, the Government has provided mortgage repayment relief of one million forints for large families when a third child is born and a further one million forints for each subsequent child. From now on, the

[48] Péter Cseresnyés. Hungary Today. 2020. [https://hungarytoday.hu/successful-family-economic-policies-family-affairs-minister-novak-hungary-at-first-site-conference/] (Accessed 11.07.22)

[49] European Large Family Confederation. 2019. [https://www.elfac.org/hungary-prime-minister-viktor-orban-announced-a-seven-point-family-protection-action-plan/] (Accessed 11.07.22)

Government will provide this relief of one million forints when a second child is born, a further HUF four million for the birth of a third child, and one million forints after every subsequent child.

4. He said that women who have given birth to and raised four or more children would be exempt from personal income tax for the rest of their lives.

5. He also introduced a car purchase programme for large families. The Government will provide families raising at least three children with a non-repayable grant of HUF 2.5 million to purchase new cars with at least seven seats.

6. Mr Orbán said that universal crèche care would be made available. For three years, 21,000 new places will be created in crèches: 10,000 this year, 5,000 in 2020 and 6,000 in 2021. It means that by 2022 every family will be able to place their young children in crèche facilities.

7. The seventh point of the action plan is the introduction of childcare payments for grandparents: if parents so decide, grandparents will be able to receive childcare payments instead of them. He also announced the modernisation of language teaching in secondary schools, enabling every secondary school student to attend two-week language courses abroad in the summer breaks of their 9th and 11th years in education.

This plan and Hungary's subsequent results have attracted international attention from other countries such as Japan, Poland and USA.

It shows that with political will, determination and competent leadership it is more than possible to turn this demographic decline around to demographic growth and reach sustainable numbers.

I worked closely with Mr. Benedict Eschö, a long term advisor to President Orban. We wanted to promote my concept of how to increase the birth rate to the government of Taiwan which has a Total Fertility Rate of 1.1 children per woman through the Hungarian Foreign Department. The project was disbanded after a short while, however to my pleasant surprise I saw the lion parts of my proposed project being used to increase the birth rates in Hungary. It pays off to get involved, even if you do not see the effects right away, you never know who will pick up your ideas and arguments and go with them further.

European and American Egocentric Viewpoint

Western life tends to focus increasingly on the individual. Politicians address themselves to egocentric issues that will draw attention and votes in an election. This path is very narrow and will end in catastrophe for Europe and America. This collapse won't occur in a big bang, but in a fading away. Westerners know a lot about their civil rights, but not enough about their civil duties.

Self-focus creates a very short-term perspective that is doomed in the long term. When one has discussions about what will happen in the future, including the idea of fading democracies with no equality, no women's rights, and no voting power, the usual answer is "Well, I haven't thought of that."

Today's youth are very much engaged with world problems, but young people have to go one step further. They must shoulder the burden that their parents have left them -they must increase the population to ensure a future for their countries. However, as we have seen in the case of Hungary, to make this a reality it is very beneficial to have government policies in place that support this.

It is also the duty of well-educated people and high income earners to have more children because their genes are needed in future generations, and they can afford it.

Now there is a tendency for non-educated people to have children, supported by social policies targeting poor and underprivileged individuals. The thoughts and values that these children are raised with will replace the values and ideals of the educated and higher classes in the US and in Europe. Thus perpetuating a mentality of dependency and poverty, as we know that the social and economic status and achievements of the offspring correlate strongly to that of the parents.

European, American and Japanese people have to understand that acting from their short-term ego will send their children to slavery and the horror of social collapse, being outcompeted and dominated by more fertile populations and more competitive authoritarian states such as China. What is the western response to this?

9. Historical view: why democracies have failed

There has been a lot of work dedicated to the historical analysis of why democracies fall to pieces. Based on research, history's democracies have been analysed and compared from a demographic point of view. Analysis shows an astonishing result. We see a red thread running through history.

In simple terms:

A good that's too good causes complacency.

This repeats itself in every democracy. The more developed the society, the faster the "liquidation process" occurs once it has started.

In this chapter you will find a listing of many democracies, starting with the old Indian societies and finishing with democracies after the Second World War. Some modern democracies have to be analysed from a more long-term perspective because time is a significant factor. However, sometimes changes come so fast that they knock out the time factor.

Democracy	Opponent
Ancient India	**Alexander the Great, king of Macedonia**
In ancient India, the society's monarchical traditions clashed with the self-governing tendencies of certain groups. According to the Vedas, there were 12 societies of the republican type in the Buddhist period of Indian history (6th century BC – 2nd century AD). Republican power was very characteristic of northwest India. In that area, there were city-states similar to the Greek ones in terms of their political structure; they were much more populated, though. Old Indian manuscripts describe a democratic procedure of decision-making that dates back to the 6-11 century BC. For instance, you can come across such terms as 'voting', 'vote-based decisions', and 'quorum ' that are close to the modern notions of these terms. There is evidence that political forces united and formed parties. Also, the texts indicate that some committees of representatives were established to deal with certain questions. Decision-making procedures were formalised so that all interests could be taken into account. India's distinctive feature combines traditional forms of power and democratic procedures that extend the population's political rights.	The Indian republics could not equal Alexander's army. His troops were reinforced with soldiers from previously conquered nations and, as a result, were stronger. It was approximately in 320 BC that the independent Indian republics finally submitted. The Indian democracy could not maintain stable population growth, and due to the invasion by nations with a higher birth rate, democracy in India collapsed.

The low birth rate led to the collapse of Indian democracy. |
| Altogether in ancient India, the level of education increased.

The standard of living increased.
The number of births decreased. | |

Democracy	Opponent
Ancient Greece (Athens)	**Sparta and Macedonia**
Greek democracy is one of the classic forms of democracy found in world history. Initially, this democracy referred to city-states that formed political units in Greece. The ancient city of Athens was the city-state with the most developed system of democratic government. It had a developed trading industry and class of craftsmen at its foundation, and its population was more educated in comparison to other city-states. Athens became a prototype for the "open society". It is traditionally believed that during Pericles's reign (443-429 BC), Athens' democracy reached its high point.	Athens and Sparta, another Greek city-state, are well-known in ancient history for their incessant confrontation. The population mostly occupied itself with agriculture. Sparta, in fact, had an almost anti-democratic government, a stronger army, and a higher birth rate. As a result, Sparta won a victory over Athens after a number of long wars. In the 6th century BC, Alexander the Great and his troops invaded Greece and made it surrender completely. Macedonia had a far more numerous population with a high birth rate. Moreover, Alexander's troops were reinforced with the people from the conquered lands. The population of Macedonia was dozens or probably hundreds of times as large as the population of Greece. The low birth rate resulted in the collapse of Greek democracy.

Democracy	Opponent
The Empire and the fall of ancient Rome Very few families in Rome had more than two children.	**Barbarians** By the 4th century AD, the Empire was shattered. The invasion of barbarians in the second half of the 5th century AD had put an end to ancient Rome and the ancient period as a whole. Rome also suffered from the growing encroachment of the poor and people from the provinces. The demographics of migration made the political situation in Rome even more complicated. It was virtually impossible to collect taxes due to an uncontrolled population flow, and this destroyed the Empire's economy. The necessary prerequisites for revolution were created, and the legitimate government weakened. The 5th century and the end of the 4th century saw a barbarian invasion. In fact, the migration and inner social processes that led to the decline of Roman civilisation were intensified by the fact that the invaders were of a lower-level of cultural background. Democracy and ancient culture overall disappeared for a long time. Low birth rates resulted in the collapse of democracy.

Democracy	Opponent
Iceland	**The Kingdom of Norway**
In the history of world democracy, Iceland is famous for its parliament, the Alting. This was the first general assembly in world history. The Alting appeared in 930. The Alting was summoned annually and was supplemented by lower-level meetings (Tings). At that time, Iceland was mostly inhabited by bonds, i.e. free people, landlords, heads of families, ploughmen, cattle breeders, hunters and sailors. Almost all the inhabitants of Iceland visited the Alting. They held it for two weeks in July. It concerned law-making, juridical proceedings, discussion of important issues and making decisions. For instance, the Alting decided to adopt Christianity in 1000 AD. Iceland was an independent democratic republic from 930 to 1262. Altogether in Iceland, the level of education increased. The number of births decreased.	In 1262, Iceland lost its independence and answered to Norway. Norway was approximately 20 Limes as populated as Iceland. As Iceland had a low birth rate, the Icelanders could not maintain democracy. Iceland's low birth rate resulted in the collapse of democracy.

Democracy	Opponent
Democracy in Novgorod, Russia	**Dutchy of Ivan the Terrible, later Tzar of Russia**
Democracy in Novgorod was based on the decisions made during a Veche. This was a general meeting that was concerned with making major decisions and appointing people to key positions in the government. The level of education increased sharply in the town of Novgorod. The standard of living also increased.	In the 16th century, the Muscovite troops of Ivan the Terrible forcibly annexed the Novgorod area and made it a pan of Muscovy. The Muscovite tsar's troops were more numerous than the Novgorod ones, and the nations that formed the Tsar's troops had a higher birth rate than in Novgorod. Consequently, the Novgorod democratic system was destroyed. A low birth rate resulted in the collapse of democracy in Novgorod.

Democracy	Opponent
Germany 1920-1930	**National Socialism (Fascism)**
The period in German history, starting with the signing of the Treaty of Versailles (1918) and up to the time when social democrats rose to power, is traditionally called the Weimar Republic. The Weimar democracy is known for its numerous political movements of various kinds and for its specific liberality. Also, German culture in this period reached its climax. The level of education and standard of living increased among intellectuals.	The primary factor that shook the Weimar Republic and eventually led to its collapse was a worldwide economic crisis that began in October 1929 and lasted till 1932-1933. The economic crisis resulted in the dismissal of Chancellor Heinrich Bruning, whose deflationary policies were widely unpopular. An end was brought to parliamentary democracy. As a result of the economic crisis, the Rightist and Leftist antidemocratic parties grew dramatically, leading to an increased number of enemies of liberty. The democratic freedom allowed by the Weimar Republic was abused by anti-democratic forces to destroy the system. On February 27, 1933, National Socialists headed by Adolph Hitler committed arson and burned down the Reichstag. It was a provocation, and in that way, the National Socialists managed to get rid of their political opponents. The period of fascism started in Germany. The state made a drastic turn toward totalitarianism and militarism. National Socialists had a very rigid fascist ideology. One of their main principles was a dramatic increase in the number of party proponents. The birth rate among fascist proponents was higher than among democrats. On average, children in Nazi families outnumbered liberal families by two. The low birth rate resulted in the collapse of democracy in Weimar, Germany.

Above, we have looked at democracies throughout history. We have already mentioned that high cultures tend to wither away when complacency, laziness, and egocentricity take over.

Marcus Cato complained in a speech to the people of Rome that one could be quite sure that the decline of the Roman Republic was imminent. He had in mind that when young men indulge themselves by paying the equivalent of $1,000 for a boy for sexual pleasure, and 300 drachmas for a jar of caviar, even though pretty boys cost more than one's monthly wages in the field, and jars of caviar cost more than the price of the ploughman, then the decline of civilisation is near.

And he was right!

And now it is the USA and Europe's turn.

10. What is chaos?

In order to explain what will happen in Old Europe and some other parts of the Western World, a short discussion about chaos is necessary.

There are certain rules that governing chaos can give us vital information about the future of Europe.

According to Gottfried Mayer-Kress, well known in academic circles for his work in kinesiology, chaos is the following:

"When we look at the changing world that we are living in, we can categorise the types of changes into a few fundamental categories: growth and recession, stagnation, cyclic behaviour and unpredictable, erratic fluctuations. All of these phenomena can be described with very well-developed linear mathematical tools. Here linear means that the result of an action is always proportional to its cause: if we double our effort, the outcome will also double. However, more is non-linear in the same sense as most zoology is non-elephant zoology. The situation that most traditional science focuses on in linear systems can be compared to the story of the person looking for the lost car keys under a street lamp because it is too dark to see anything where the keys were lost.

Only recently do we have access to methods and computing power to make significant progress in the field of nonlinear systems and understand, for example, seemingly simple things like dripping faucets. One whole class of phenomena, which does not exist within the framework of linear theory, has become known under the buzzword of chaos. The modern notion of chaos describes irregular and highly complex structures in time and space following deterministic laws and equations. This is in contrast to the structure less chaos of traditional equilibrium thermodynamics. The basic example system that might be helpful for visualisation is fluid on a stove, with the stress level given by the rate at which the fluid is heated. We can see that the closer the system comes to equilibrium, the less spatial structure. The dynamics of the individual subsystem are random and without spatial or temporal coherence. Beyond a given threshold of external stress, the system starts to self-organize and forms regular spatial patterns (rolls, hexagons), which create coherent behaviour of the subsystems ('order parameters slave sub systems'). The order parameters themselves do not evolve in time. Under increasing stress, the order parameters begin to oscillate in an organised manner: We have coherent and ordered dynamics of the subsystems. Further increase of the external stress leads to bifurcation and more complicated temporal behaviour, but the system is still acting coherently. This continues until the system shows deterministic temporal chaos. The dynamics are now predictable only for a finite time. This predictability time depends on the degree of chaos present in the system. It will decrease as the system becomes more chaotic. The spatial coherence of the system will be destroyed, and independent subsystems will emerge which will interact and create temporary coherent structures."

There is frequent confusion between chaos and randomness. There are some similarities in the nature of a chaotic and a random system, but there are also some fundamental differences.

Some of them are listed here:

Discrimination table between Order, Chaos and Randomness

System	Order	Chaos	Randomness
Paradigmatic Example	Clocks, Planets	Clouds, Weather	Snow on TV Screen
Predictability	Very High	Finite, Short Term	None -> Simple Laws
Effect of Small Errors	Very Small	Explosive	Nothing BUT Errors
Spectrum	Pure	Yes	Noisy, Broad
Dimension	Finite	Low	Infinite Infinite
Control	Easy	Tricky, Very Effective	Poor
Attractor	Point, Cycle, Strange	Strange, Fractal	No

Table 6: Order, Chaos and Randomness

Organisation of Chaos and Turbulence

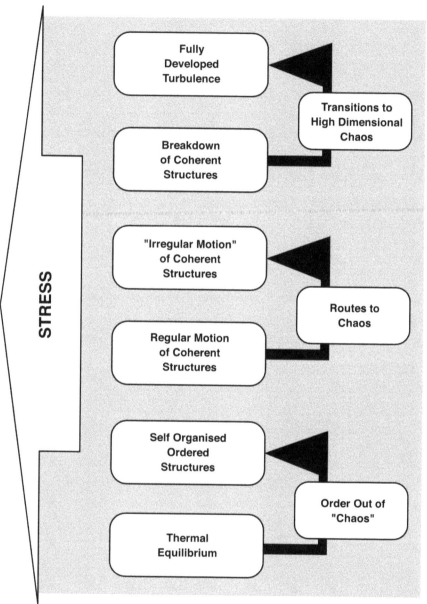

Ill. 7: Chaos and Turbulence

Stress = Continued change at an Increased rate.

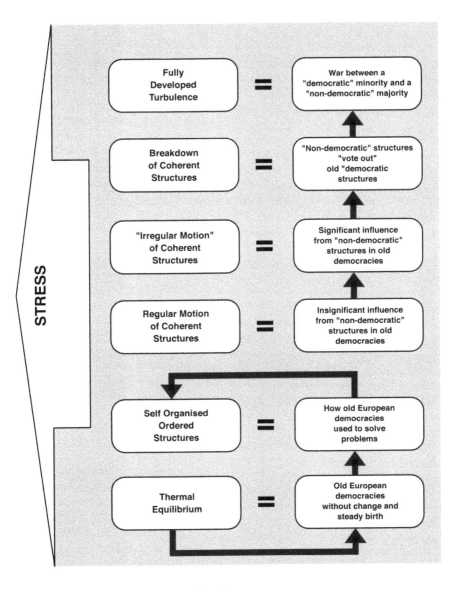

Ill. 8: Structures

According to chaos theory, we foresee that Old Europe will go from order to chaos and that fully developed turbulence will lead to a civil war in Europe.

The governing cliques in Old Europe will not notice this chaos until it is too late. Progressive ideology and hunger for power and prestige are blinding the European politicians who could otherwise make vital changes.

The final product will be a rigorous control. A well-controlled Europe will continuously check everybody by using a new "progressive religion" or massive electronic surveillance, or both. Perhaps the civil war in Europe will be so disastrous that we will return to a non-scientific society.

From the theory, we predict a collapsing economy and the end of the free press and democracy, while strife and civil war will engulf Old Europe.

11. Philosophical approach

A fascinating question is: how did this European ego fixation come about?

When did it start? Is egoism the reason why societies and especially democracies, tend to fall? What are the philosophical arguments about this development? Or did the philosophers not recognise this development?

The French philosopher Descartes argued that: "Cogito ergo sum", that is: "I think, therefore I exist".

This helped create the concept of the separate individual and put us on the path toward the ego-centred, atomised, individualistic worldview. The underlying meaning behind this statement is that each individual thinks for themself and not jointly with somebody else. This Descartesian statement became the start of a new pattern in Western thought.

Imanuel Kant (1724-1804), from Konigsberg, was next. He introduced the human mind as an active originator of experience rather than just a passive recipient of perception.

Kant believed in common concepts of perception consciousness (Bewusstsein) and perception (Wahrnehmung) and said: I know, I think, I see, I remember it all belongs to my consciousness, in one temporal stream of experience.

During Kant's time, the underpopulation problem was not significant in Europe. Europe had started to implement modern medicine and hygiene. The number of people increased each year.

For Kant, personal experience was most important. He was concerned with how each individual developed his ego. Kant also developed four types of individual egos. Kant built a fantastic system of thought and significantly impacted Western thinking. There have even been discussions to rename the city Konigsberg (Kaliningrad) to Kantgrad.

Kant's ideas became the origin of positivism. The positivists stressed humanity's significant advances in biology, economics, and social progress.

In many areas, humankind took over. Darwin's theories completely changed the concept of man's evolution and pushed into the background religious ideas that had been dominant.

Democracy was on the move. Freedom was an essential idea of all, and in particular, Freedom of the individual. Auguste Comte (1798-1857), who came from Montpellier in France, argued that evolution had three stages: theological, metaphysical, and positive. Comte believed that freedom would free the science of sociology from the theological and metaphysical prejudices that still blocked it.

The English positivist Herbert Spencer is considered the systematiser of positivism according to the principles of evolution. Spencer also stressed the individual ego and concentration that leads to even more complacency.

Hegel borrowed many concepts from Kant and developed the basis for German idealism.

From Hegel, we have two wings, the left and right-wing. The left-wing, as represented by Marx and Engels, is well-known. These men's ideas were used to grab power and then, in a very self-centred way, concentrate total control in the hands of very few. On Hegel's right-wing, we have Hackel. Ernst Heinrich Hackel (1834-1919), was a materialist in the true sense. Man is, like all other beings, a compound of matter and energy. God is the sum of all forces acting in the universe (Please look at the chapter on chaos).

These thinkers became the ideological foundation that modern European thoughts were based.

Critics of positivism

There were and still are many critics of these thought patterns. Soren Kierkegaard (1813-1855) vehemently criticised Hegel's system of philosophy in his work "Afsluttende uvidenskabelig Efterskrift", roughly translated as "A Concluding Unscientific Postscript" (just as our book is, in a way, unscientific). In this "Postscript", Kierkegaard attacked all philosophical system building and formulated the thesis that subjectivity is truth. Each individual is free to choose their truth based on the subjectivity of this individual's Liker Dostoyevsky (1821-1881) attacked the materialistic West in "Notes from the Underground" (1864). Friedrich Nietzsche (1844-1900) also confronted Western philosophy in his work "Umwertungaller Werte" in a way no other author had done before.

Ludwig Wittgenstein (1889-1951), a professor at Cambridge University, took influences from the cultural and historical philosopher Oswald Spengler, the biggest doomsday prophet of them all, and from the scientist Ludwig Boltzman. Oswald Spengler has also influenced contemporary writers and thinkers such as Samuel Phillips Huntington, an American political scientist who is best known for his thesis and book "The Clash of Civilizations and the Remaking of World Order", where he argues that cultural and religious identities will be the source of future conflict now that the Cold War is over; competing civilisations will clash together, and there is no guarantee the West will stay on top.

Finnish philosopher George Henrik von Wright (1916-2003 Helsinki), also a Cambridge professor, asked Wittgenstein in 1939 if there would be a war. Wittgenstein answered that there would be two or three.

I fully agree with Ludwig Wittgenstein that there will be another world war. For this reason, refer to the chapter in this book entitled "What will happe". To summarise that chapter here, the populations of democratic countries will slowly die off because they do not breed enough. Other competing countries and civilisations will rise to fill the vacuum left by the west and trigger a conflict.

Von Wright speaks about the advances Western society has made, and he uses the term "provocative pessimism" to underline his approach toward Western stigmatism. It all comes down to the Western world, with all its scientists and pragmatic positivists, looking only at the short-term and focusing on a limited number of factors typically explained using a linear graph. Only a minimal number of the world's events are linear. The rest are much more complex and are better described by fractals. Fractals are used to explain chaos. See the previous chapter on "What is chaos".

Today's problem is that reality is becoming increasingly complex, and no politician, scientist, philosopher, or human being can cover all subjects. Of course, some politicians say that they can, but they lie. Most of us ordinary people do not have the expert's view on all subjects, and thus democracy will suffer as the world becomes more complex and people begin to lack knowledge in a variety of fields.

We have already stated that people from democratic societies with liberal education have fewer children; thus, democracy is doomed from this point of view. In contrast to religion, democracy does not have rules for handling many important long-term questions. The low birth rate is one such problem. Religious thought addresses the birth rate issue, one reason why religions survive for thousands of years while democracies and well-off societies that fall into complacency and narcissism fade away much sooner.

The best example of a surviving religion is the Indus culture, followed by the Hindu religion. This culture has survived for over 5,000 years, and it developed two democracies, one that lasted for about 3,000 years and the other that was crushed by Alexander the Great. The winner takes all.

The Indus religion combined a stable life with a fertility culture. Even if the standard of living soared (see Alexander Tytler's graph), the Indus culture increased the fertility of the civilisation, both in quantity (many people) and in quality (high standard of living). Do not forget that today there are 300 million people in India living at the same level as Europeans, even though CNN and other media will show you the 800-900 million poor people to raise your ego. India is also making reforms. Whether India's reforms are for good or bad, we'll see.

If India can preserve its religion, the country may succeed. Religions have many rules which help them to survive. These rules are not available in a democracy because most people cannot become experts in all areas. It is impossible to know everything. In some religions, this knowledge is embedded, at least partly. Democracies need to learn from religions how to safeguard long term development that can warrant all achievements, at least those that might be long-lasting. There has to be a split between those topics to be determined in elections and those that need long-term solutions.

Many cultures without a written language survive longer than those with a written one. Why? Because the written word usually serves those in power. Having the power to become an omnipotent dictatorship. That is what happened when Eve took a bite of the apple from the tree of knowledge.

12. Biological approach

Is it natural to have children? I think most people would answer yes to this question. It may be the most natural way of expressing love. Historically, families had several children, especially when child mortality rates were high. In the past, one had to have several children so that some of them would survive. What biological effects does childbirth have on both the individual and society as a whole?

We know that a woman undergoes significant changes in her hormonal structure while pregnant. She prepares for her role as a mother and feels close to the unborn child. She becomes more caring.

Lately, a group of scientists at Memorial and Queens Universities in Canada, led by the psychologist Anne Storey and professor of biology Katherine E Wynne-Edwards, has started to research what happens to three hormones in the male body when their mate becomes pregnant. The scientists monitored the level of three hormones, Prolactin, Cortisol, and Testosterone. Scientists know that these hormones change in a woman when she is pregnant.

Prolactin is produced in the brain in hypophysis. Prolactin affects the breast, helping it to produce milk, which increases the woman's caring instinct. But the Canadian scientists found that the level of Prolactin also increased in the man by about 20% in the three weeks before the baby's birth. The Canadian scientists also found that the kidney hormone Cortisol, a stress hormone, makes a woman react more sensitive to her baby's cries – a phenomenon also found in the man. This hormone makes the man more caring.

What happened to the most famous hormone, Testosterone, which fuels aggressiveness, extroversion, and sexuality in males?

The Canadian scientists found that the level of Testosterone fell by 33% during the first three weeks after the birth of the man's child. Usually, the level of Testosterone returns to the original level after a couple of months. Sometimes it stays low. This could be to tie the father to his child throughout life.

The Canadian findings track with the findings of anthropologist Mr Peter Gray from Harvard University, who declares that the level of Testosterone decreases in fathers as compared to single men.

What do we learn from this? In European society, the single person family typically accounts for about half of all European family arrangements. This means that many men do not develop these hormonal changes related to childbirth and thus are less likely to develop strong, caring instincts.

It is better for society when men develop more social and caring instincts, the result of making their mates pregnant. This way, a man becomes more interested in society and increasingly concerned about what will happen to the tribe or country.

We can expect egoism to flourish in a society composed of people living as singles without children. The singles will continue to think of themselves, and when they grow older, they will become even more ego-focused.

A society dominated by older persons that have not developed these levels of "socially-responsible hormones" will be doomed to fail.

You fail to enter the next step of maturity by not having children, which is as important as becoming a sexual individual.

The only conclusion is that the West, especially European society, is facing a biological and sociological bankruptcy.

A birth might bring hormonal changes that are good for societal stability.

13. Remember: You are responsible!

This table has been put together after discussions with different Western persons whom I asked to discuss the future of Western culture and who commented on having more children. When conducting such discussions, you must remember that you ask a lot from a person who has no children to change their life after just a 10-minute discussion.

The western approach to becoming a parent

age	Amount of children	Western approach	Becoming a parent	Argumentation
20-30 years	During this age, "no-kid" persons will find any excuse not to have children since this would endanger their social position and reduce the amount of money they can spend on themselves. Children? OK. But later, not now. These people will find every excuse not to change their position. Having children is a distant plan. The question of becoming a parent has been subconsciously put off for many years.	The experience of becoming a parent might be so turbulent that the bare thought of having more children will scare them. Men might have felt the suppressing power of women and the huge burden from society once they became parents.	These persons will probably agree with the idea of 2. 1 child per woman because they already have two children and have the time to have more children. They also want a secure future for their kids; therefore, they will support the idea of a 2.1 child as a minimum survival level.	"Oh, you have so many children at such a young age?" some say to the young bearers. Some say it jealously. Some say it admiringly. The problem for these families is that they are not getting enough social support. Some big families realise their happiness and want to have even more children.

age	Amount of children	Western approach	Becoming a parent	Argumentation
30-40 years	During this age, persons with no children are having an internal fight. The ego-focused person is often caught up in a career that bars them from having children. The biological clock is ticking, but the brain is blocked by egoism.	"One child is enough," people in this category often say. Having a child was a huge problem, but now it's over. They usually "drug" themselves with work, career and friends to avoid the question.	A stable, common family type that fits the usual standard. We are two people. We have two children. We have done our duty. They might become irritated when you say that 2. 1 child per couple is needed. Many of these families or persons do not want to have another child. Still, some in this group will see the need because they are coming closer to pension age.	These persons will welcome discussion because they are above the 2.1 children per woman/couple. They also see the need for the future.
40 ->	Now it is becoming late. Rather late. Now the biological clock is ticking louder. Many women in highly industrialised countries give birth to their first baby when they have turned 40. Many men have already accepted the fact that they will never have children.	"Another child, after so many years?" Oh, no. One child will do. I do not want to change my life just to have one more child.	These people see the need for 2. 1 child per woman to safeguard their pensions and healthcare.	These persons feel secure because they have a backup regarding the future of healthcare in Europe. These people will receive healthcare through their children when social healthcare fails.

Table 7: Argumentation table

14. Case Studies

14.1 Texas: A White Minority Reality

"Whites will be a minority" is something you stumble upon from time to time when you listen to or read demographic-related news or read about immigration online.

We see this trend in all Western countries with an open border policy. What was regarded as a "racist conspiracy theory"[50] is today widely acknowledged among many official governmental institutions. This is especially the case in countries such as the U.S., where it is still legal and not so controversial to talk about race or to make statistics relevant to demographic trends among the population.

While it is troublesome to know that whites are on the way to becoming a minority on national levels in their homelands, many forget that whites already are a minority, depending on where you look. On a global scale, whites have been a minority for a while now, but inside their traditional homelands, they have already become a minority locally in certain regions. This is how the trend of whites becoming a minority in their homelands will play out; locally, region by region, they will be crowded out. This phenomenon is also known as "white flight".

For example, in the U.S., whites are already a minority in certain states, ironically sometimes referred to as "majority-minority" states. According to the U.S. Census Bureau, whites are now (apart from Hawaii) a minority in New Mexico, California, Nevada and Texas, which will be the showcase example in this article. The reason we chose Texas for this case study is not only because the demographic change is evident in that area but also because Texas is generally perceived as being a quite traditional, Christian and Republican state in the U.S.

---

[50] Odette, Yousef. 2022. The 'great replacement' conspiracy theory isn't fringe anymore, it's mainstream. npr. [https://www.npr.org/2022/05/17/1099233034/the-great-replacement-conspiracy-theory-isnt-fringe-anymore-its-mainstream] (Accessed 11.07.22)

A closer look at Texas demographic statistics

Before The Immigration and Nationality Act of 1965

According to the Census Bureau, 87.4% identified themselves as white in 1960[51], five years before The Immigration and Nationality Act of 1965. Sometimes Hispanics or other mixed raced non-whites can be included in the "white category" whenever you look at US statistics, but even if some Hispanics were to be included in those statistics, it is clear that the white population undoubtedly constituted the majority of the population in the state of Texas. This was before the multicultural-ideology era, and the immigration act of 1965 was imposed, so it makes sense that the population was still majority white.

How has the trend been since The Immigration and Nationality Act of 1965?

To get an insight into the demographic situation in Texas one can simply visit the official website of the Texas Department of State Health Services[52].

If we start by looking approximately 30 years past the establishment of The Immigration and Nationality Act of 1965, we can already see a drastic change in the racial demographics. In 1998, whites constituted 57,6% of the population in Texas. Even though whites were still a majority in 1998, it can not be denied that a roughly 30% decrease over 33 years is a radical change. One of the main factors behind this change was, of course, a liberal immigration policy and a significant increase in the Hispanic population, who by this time consisted of almost a third of the people in Texas (28,3%).

---

[51] Campbell Gibson and Kay Jung 2002. Historical Census Statistics on Population Totals By Race, 1790 to 1990, and By Hispanic Origin, 1970 to 1990, For The United States, Regions, Divisions. U.S. Census Bureau [https://www.census.gov/content/dam/Census/library/working-papers/2002/demo/POP-twps0056.pdf] (Accessed 11.07.22)

[52] Texas Department of State Health Services [https://www.dshs.texas.gov/chs/popdat/default.shtml] (Accessed 11.07.22)

Texas Demographics

According to the most recent ACS, the racial composition of Texas in 2022 was:

- White: 69.16%
- Black or African American: 12.10%
- Two or more races: 6.98%
- Other race: 6.25%
- Asian: 4.94%
- Native American: 0.48%
- Native Hawaiian or Pacific Islander: 0.09%
- https://worldpopulationreview.com/states/texas-population

Here we see a VERY different picture, not distorted by the Mainstream Media:

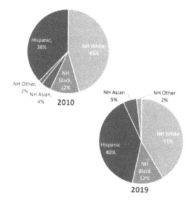

Race/Ethnicity	2019 Population Estimate
NH White	11,950,774
Hispanic	11,525,578
NH Black	3,501,610
NH Asian	1,457,549
NH Two or More Races	425,866
NH American Indian & Alaska Native	94,168
NH Native Hawaiian & Other Pacific Islander	25,861

Ill. 9: Texas Demographics[53]

---

[53] Texas Demographic Trends and Projections. [https://demographics.texas.gov/Resources/Presentations/OSD/2021/2021_01_29_MexicanAmericanLegislativeLeadershipFellowship.pdf] (Accessed 19.10.22)

It is not a coincidence that the states closest to the Mexican border are the states that are the first to experience the consequences of mass immigration in terms of demographics. Suppose we fast forward to 2017, almost 60 years since The Immigration and Nationality Act of 1965. In that case, we can now confirm that whites are not only a minority. They are not even the biggest minority group in the State of Texas (whites comprise 40,9% compared to the Hispanic population of 41%). This shows how rapidly opening border policies can change an entire population. Not even a century has passed, but white people now make up less than half of the population, compared to 87,4% in 1960.

Conclusion

Of course, Texas is just one showcase example; however, we can observe the same trend occurring not only in pretty much all states in the U.S. but in all white majority countries that adapt to the multicultural agenda. The only difference is the rate, i.e. what year this demographic shift is expected to happen. Whether in 2050, 2060, or a few decades later is less important.

Texas is an excellent example of how "The Great Replacement" is not an ambiguous "conspiracy theory" or something that might happen in some distant future in theory; it is a phenomenon that is not only real but is happening here and now.

14.2 The Current State of Sweden

The Demographic Future With Current Policies

Sweden is a Scandinavian country with just over ten million inhabitants[54]. Although Sweden is sparsely populated, around 85% of the population lives in urbanised areas. Most live in the southern coastal regions, where the climate is less harsh.

The descendants of Vikings have left their Norse pagan traditions behind and turned to Christianity. The nation became Christian in the 12th

---

[54] Sweden Population 2022 (Live). World Population Review. [https://worldpopulationreview.com/countries/sweden-population] (Accessed 11.07.22)

century, and turned to Protestantism around the 16th century. Nowadays, around 70% of the population continues to be registered as Christian, even though the Swedish people are not very religious.

Swedish Fertility

The fertility rate in Sweden is relatively high. With a score of 1.67 births per woman (2022 est.)[55], it is ranked 2nd in the EU. Nonetheless, it is still below the replacement rate of 2.1, so any population growth in Sweden is necessarily due to immigration.

A more detailed view shows a significant difference in fertility rates between Muslims and non-Muslims in Sweden[56]. Muslims have an average rate of 2.8. For non-Muslims, the rate is below 1. 67. In other words, Muslim women have, on average, one child more than other women.

The Foreign-Born Population

Approximately one in six inhabitants is foreign-born. That translates into about 17% or 1.7 million people.

---

[55] Sweden Total fertility rate. cia.gov. [https://www.cia.gov/the-world-factbook/countries/sweden/#people-and-society] (Accessed 11.07.22)

[56] In Europe, Muslims projected to have more children than non-Muslims. 2017. Pew Research Center. [https://www.pewresearch.org/religion/2017/11/29/europes-growing-muslim-population/pf_11-29-17_muslims-update-16/] (Accessed 11.07.22)

Origin of the foreign-born Swedes.

	Women	Men	Both
Finland	94,077	61,968	156,045
Irak	61,073	70,815	131,888
Syria	41,515	56,701	98,216
Polen	46,907	38,610	85,517
Iran	33,126	35,941	69,067
Jugoslavia	33,382	33,808	67,190
Somalia	30,329	30,294	60,623
Bosnia Hercegovina	29,172	28,533	57,705
Germany	26,174	23,412	49,586
Turkey	20,853	25,520	46,373
Norway	23,387	18,687	42,074
Denmark	19,653	22,217	41,870
Thailand	30,349	8,443	38,792
Afghanistan	12,558	18,709	31,267
Eritrea	12,724	15,892	28,616
Total	848,237	828,027	1,676,264

Table 8: Foreign-born Swedes[57]

Note: The data above is slightly outdated. Syria has since overtaken Finland as the number one spot, due to the war in Syria and subsequent refugee crisis, where Sweden took in a record number of Syrian-born refugees.

If we look not at foreign-born, but foreign-background, we include those born in Sweden to parents that migrated there.

---

[57] Number of persons with foreign or Swedish background (rough division) by region, age and sex. Year 2002 - 2021. Statistics Service [https://www.statistikdatabasen.scb.se/pxweb/en/ssd/START__BE__BE0101__BE0101Q/UtlSvBakgGrov/?rxid=ad763246-c0fa-4631-9fa2-a7326aa73af0] (Accessed 11.07.22)

Those numbers are shared in an online database open for search to the public. It shows us that in 2017, 24% of the population currently living in Sweden had a foreign background. Or about 2.4 million people.

2017 Foreign background:

- Men 1.229.334
- Women 1.209.673

In the age group 15-24, the percentage of foreign background is 30%[57]. The younger generations have a higher percentage of immigrants, while the older generations have fewer migrants. It is this category that will produce the next cohort of babies born. Thus, we can assume that 1 in 3 babies born will be to parents from a foreign background. One in three is slightly more than 30%; however, fertility rates among these groups are also higher than among native Swedes. Taking that into account, one in three is a conservative estimate.

The Inflow of More Migrants

In 2015, Sweden received 163.000[58] asylum migrants, a large part from Syria. That equals a 10% increase in the foreign-born population in a year or a 1.6% increase in the country's overall population. That is a larger number than the total number of babies born in Sweden in any given year.

In 2008, a mere 60% of the foreign-born population was employed. This compares bleakly to 80% of the Swedish-born population. The overall effect on public expenditure has been a net loss, despite the population increase resulting in higher GDP.

---

58 Traub, James. 2021. Even Sweden Doesn't Want Migrants Anymore. FOREIGN POLICY. [https://foreignpolicy.com/2021/11/17/even-sweden-doesnt-want-migrants-anymore-syria-iraq-belarus/] (Accessed 11.07.22)

Islam in Sweden

Currently 8.1% of the Swedish population is Islamic. Depending on the rate of immigration, expectations[59] are that by 2050 this portion will be between 11% and 30%. The 11% estimate would be with zero immigration. The 30% would be the case with immigration levels similar to recent years.

The 30% would mean 4.4 million Muslims in Sweden by 2050, compared to under a million now.

The Maths

Every year, 115.000 babies are born in Sweden. Two out of three will be likely born to Swedish parents, so 77.000. The other 38.000 will descend from foreign backgrounds. Although in 2015 the number of migrants was 163.000, this year was an exception. In 2014 there were 80.000. It has since dropped to approximately 30.000 for 2016 and 2017.

However, even with the lower numbers, we have 30.000 newcomers annually. Add that with the 38.000 children born to parents with a foreign-background, and we get 68.000. The number of native born children is 77.000.

So yearly, there are 145.000 new inhabitants of Sweden. Just over half of those have Swedish backgrounds, while the rest are from foreign backgrounds. As the migrants are generally younger and of child-rearing age, we can expect their share in new births to increase over time. Nearly half of the Swedish population growth is due to foreigners already.

If fertility rates and migration numbers remain stable, we can make a simple prediction for the future of Sweden. Once the children born in 2017 grow up and start having children of their own, the 77.000 Swedes of the

[59] Europe's Growing Muslim Population. 2017. PEW RESEARCH CENTER. [https://www.pewresearch.org/religion/2017/11/29/europes-growing-muslim-population/] (Accessed 11.07.22)

2017 cohort will have about 69.000 children at a fertility rate of 1.8. The 38.000 foreign backgrounds will have about 38.000 children, given a slightly increased fertility rate on average to account for the higher rate among Muslims. In addition, the 30.000 migrants from the same year will also have children; let's give a low estimate of 32.000 children. In reality, this birth rate is likely higher, due to most of them being of Muslim background, but let's keep the estimate conservative. The estimate of 32.000 children depends on a rate of 2.1 versus an actual Muslim rate of 2.8.

So, in this future wave of babies born, we estimate 69.000 are Swedes, and at least 70.000 are non-Swedes. So, in a single generation, if Sweden continues the way it is going right now, native Swedes will be a minority among babies born. From that moment on, it is only a matter of time for Swedes to become a minority overall.

In 2018 Statistiska centralbyrån (SCB)[60] presented new population statistics, and it shows that the demographic changes in Sweden continue as unabated as they are fast. The immigrant population now makes up 18.5 per cent – 1,877,050 people – of the total population.

At the beginning of 2017, the country passed ten million inhabitants, and during the year the population increased by 125,089 people, of whom 69,315 were men and 55,774 were women.

Almost 80 per cent of the growth is due to immigration and the gender imbalance is large. A total of 144,489 people immigrated, of whom 77,865 were men and 66,624 women, while 45,620 people emigrated.

In the recent 2022 election in Sweden ethnic Swedes were a minority among first-time voters for the first time in the country's history[61].

---

[60] 2018. Flera miljongränser passerades under 2017. Statistikmyndigheten SCB. [https://www.scb.se/hitta-statistik/statistik-efter-amne/befolkning/befolkningens-sammansattning/befolkningsstatistik/pong/statistiknyhet/folkmangd-och-befolkningsforandringar-2017/] (Accessed 11.07.22)

[61] 2022. Det svenske valget: Etniske svensker en minoritet blant årets førstegangs-velgere. Document.no. [https://www.document.no/2022/09/06/etniske-svensker-en-minoritet-blant-arets-forstegangsvelgere/] (Accessed 4.10.22)

Currently there are about 7,5 million voters in Sweden. Among these about 1,2 million voters were born in foreign countries. In this election there were almost 440.000 first-time voters in total, and the majority of these were of foreign origin. Historically speaking first-time voters have consisted of individuals reaching legal age since the previous election, but in 2022 the majority of new voters were immigrants. Approximately 272.000 of the first-time voters had received Swedish citizenship since the last election in 2018, making them the majority among the first-time voters. Even among first-time voters that are born in Sweden the effects of the ongoing immigration is noticeable as every fourth new voter in this group have two immigrant parents that were born abroad.

These numbers are from the national parliamentary election. In local elections among counties and municipalities Swedish citizenship is not even required, it is enough to have resided in Sweden for at least three years or more. This means that more than 600.000 foreign citizens had the right to vote in Swedish local elections in 2022.

These numbers very clearly showcase the real world effects of the ongoing population replacement. If this trend is allowed to keep on then soon there will be more voters of foreign origin in Sweden than native Swedes. And if that happens, will Sweden remain Sweden? Who benefits from this? And who will lose from this?

It is interesting to observe that the Swedish newspaper Dagens Nyheter celebrates this demographic trend and the effort to encourage foreing first-time voters to vote in the election in Sweden. This fits well with the larger trend observed internationally among the liberal media outlets. They are reporting that foreing first-time voters in Sweden are enticed with free pizza if they go and vote[62].

At the same time we can also observe a shift in the behaviour among native Swedish first-time voters and young voters in general. In this recent election in 2022 it shows that younger native Swedish voters voted predominantly concervative, giving their support to political parties

---

[62] 2022. Kan gratis pizza få fler unga på Järva att rösta?. Dagens Nyheter. [https://www.dn.se/sverige/kan-gratis-pizza-fa-fler-unga-pa-jarva-att-rosta/] (Accessed 11.09.22)

championing much more restrictive immigration policies. It looks like young native Swedes are slowly becoming more ethnically aware. What we are witnessing is the building up of a political division and conflict along ethnic and generational lines. And this is all due to the greed and ideological blindness that has captivated the current ruling establishment. This should not come as a surprise as young voters are the ones who have to live with this ongoing irresponsible immigration policy and suffer the long term consequences.

It is however a tremendous shock and a devastating blow to the self-image of the internationalist oriented press and left leaning parties in Sweden. Liberals and the left has long prided itself on being the representatives of the young and chic. They have built their image and power on this. The establishment told us for decades that the youth is our only hope, and that we should listen to the young; especially to astroturfed activists such as Greta Thunberg.

In light of this recent election and other developments in Sweden we can see that youth movements, such as the one surrounding Greta Thunberg, were just a projection from the establishment and pure PR fabrication; not an authentic and sincere grass-root movement. The revealed preference of young native Swedes tells a very different story. The liberal newspaper Göteborgs-Posten, in a rare moment of self-awareness, reports in one of their editorials that there is a huge dissonance between the perceived reality of the ideological "chattering classes" and the visceral reality that many young native swedes are experiencing every day[63].

Put together from three different political parties[64], the conservative right in Sweden received a total of 53% of the votes from first-time voters in the age group 18-22 years old. In addition to this the smaller libertarian-right party received about 5% from this age group, bringing the total to

---

[63] Cwejman, Adam. 2022. Generation Greta finns bara på kultursidorna. Göteborgs-Posten. [https://www.gp.se/ledare/generation-greta-finns-bara-p%C3%A5-kultursidorna-1.80901697] (Accessed 11.09.22)

[64] These three different parties on the conservative centre-right in Sweden are called Moderaterna (The Moderates), Kristdemokraterna (The Christian Democrats) and Sverigedemokraterna (The Sweden Democrats).

58%. They also received 52% of the votes from voters in the age group 22-30 years old. To further underscore this point; in the school-elections[65] these three parties received 57% of the votes, and the libertarian-right party received 4% on top of that.

These three parties consist of Moderaterna (The Moderates), Kristdemokraterna (The Christian Democrats) and Sverigedemokraterna (The Sweden Democrats). They all purport to be more restrictive on immigration and to be more natalist than the alternatives on the left. This is especially true for the Sverigedemokraterna (The Sweden Democrats).

To put this in contrast; only 5% of Mrs. Thunberg's peers voted for the Green Party.

Where do they settle?

These changes are more noticeable because migrants don't spread out evenly across the country. The biggest hotspots for migrants are Malmö and Stockholm. Even within those cities, they group in the suburbs. You can walk through the centre of Malmö without noticing much of the change, but go into the suburbs, and you will not recognise that you are in Sweden.

As the migrant population increases, they will spread more and more, and Swedes will more and more start to notice the changes around them.

On a positive note

The Swedish people increasingly recognise the demographic issue. For example, recently, the newly established party Alternative for Sweden[66] raised the issue of Swedes becoming a minority within a few decades and

---

[65] School-elections are mock elections to teach kids and students about how voting and elections work. They are often regarded as an indicator of the political sentiment among the youth.

[66] Alternativ för Sverige. [https://alternativforsverige.se/] (Accessed 11.07.22)

referred to it as a population replacement in one of their public speeches[67], vowing to stop it if they get the required parliamentary power. The statement was met with cheers and applause, indicating that Sweden's people are more aware of the demographic issue.

14.3 From Revolution to De-Evolution - France

The Colonies Strike Back – The Origin of French Immigration

France was, since its foundation, one of the greatest powers on the European continent. Germany and Italy did not become states until the 19th century, and only in 1871 did Germany show it was the new primary power. Although Napoleon showed that France could be stopped by a grand coalition, that did not stop the French thirst for expansion. So, as others had done before them, France started to carve up its part of the world. It conquered most of North-Western Africa, who speaks French to this day as a result.

France had colonies outside of Africa as well. However, its settlements in America were sold to the United States in the Louisiana Purchase. Beyond that, France had a small presence in Asia, ending with the Vietnamese revolting in the 1950s leading up to the Vietnam War. By far, France's colonial presence was centred on Africa.

This is also where most of France's migrants come from, similar to the current situation in the UK, where the largest portion of migrants come from ex-colony countries, such as Pakistan and India. Fueled by relaxed immigration rules for those coming from the previous colonial territory and the ease of already speaking the language, masses of Africans moved to France in search of a more comfortable life.

---

[67] AFS: "Det sker ett folkutbyte i Sverige – som vi tänker stoppa!" 2018. FT News Group OÜ. [https://www.friatider.se/afs-det-sker-ett-folkutbyte-i-sverige-som-vi-t-nker-stoppa] (Accessed 11.07.22)

The Demographics of France

There are about 67 million[68] inhabitants in France. Using the percentages below[69], this implies less than sixty million French-born citizens, versus another eight million[70] foreigners and foreign-born. If we include the descendants of immigrant parents, we have another 6.5 million[71] more. That would bring us to 20% of the citizens of France being immigrants or born from immigrant parents. This would leave around 53 million of the total 67 million being born to parents that were also born in France.

Population of France, 2014

Considering France has an unemployment[72] rate of 8%. It is hard to argue all those eight million are there to fill the empty vacancies. This becomes even more visible when we realise that 17% of the foreign-born[73] population is unemployed, more than double the national average. This means that a disproportionate amount of the foreign-born population is welfare receivers compared to the rest of the inhabitants of France.

[68] Total population of France from 1982 to 2021, in millions. 2022. Statista. [https://www.statista.com/statistics/459939/population-france/] (Accessed 11.07.22)

[69] Share of the population in France in 2020, by nationality status. 2022. Statista. [https://www.statista.com/statistics/466028/distribution-population-nationality-france/] (Accessed 11.07.22)

[70] Foreign-born population of France from 2009 to 2020. 2022. Statista. [https://www.statista.com/statistics/548869/foreign-born-population-of-france/] (Accessed 11.07.22)

[71] Which Countries Do French Immigrants Originate From? worldatlas.com. (https://www.worldatlas.com/articles/where-do-french-immigrants-come-from.html) (Accessed 11.07.22)

[72] France: Unemployment rate from 1991 to 2021. Statista. 2022. [https://www.statista.com/statistics/263697/unemployment-rate-in-france/] (Accessed 11.07.22)

[73] Foreign-born unemployment. Organisation for Economic Co-operation and Development. [https://data.oecd.org/migration/foreign-born-unemployment.htm#indicator-chart] (Accessed 11.07.22)

France's population is expected to grow[74] to over 72 million by 2050. This makes it one of a few European countries that is expected to grow at all. Since Europe has fertility rates below the replacement rate of 2.1, any growth is purely due to immigration and a higher fertility rate among the immigrant population. France, interestingly, has a fertility rate of 1.96. That is the highest score in all of Europe, but still not high enough to explain any population growth. In fact, without immigration, it would mean France's population would shrink very slowly.

Every year there are close to 800.000 babies born in France. That number includes babies born in France by parents born outside of France. Population growth is ensured by the annual arrival of another 200.000 immigrants entering the country.

Where do France's Immigrants Come From?

As with every EU member-state, many immigrants come from other European countries. Portuguese, Italians, Germans and British all settled in France. Especially since the crisis of 2008, Europeans started moving around looking for jobs. Portugal is the biggest supplier of immigrants, with an estimated 600.000 residing in France. However, these are not all immigrants. Out of the nearly six million immigrants in France, only two million are from Europe. That leaves four million born outside of not only the EU, but outside of Europe as a whole. As mentioned previously, many of them come from Africa and/or ex-French colonies.

Exact figures regarding demographics are difficult to pinpoint since French law forbids taking an official census based on race or religion. That being said, independent research organisations are allowed to take surveys and make estimates.

- 85% French or European
- 10% North-African / Maghrebi
- 3% Sub-Saharan African
- 1.5% Asian

---

[74] What If Europe Experiences Population Decline? 2018. Clovis Institute. [http://www.clovisinstitute.org/population-decline/] (Accessed 11.07.22)

Estimates from 2009 placed the amount of Maghrebi a bit lower, at just over 5% of the total population. The North Africans are primarily Algerians and Moroccans, who comprise the largest immigrant groups from non-European origins.

Churches Are Replaced By Mosques

The independent research organisation, Pew Research, estimates the current amount of Muslims[75] in the country to be 8.8%, the highest level within the European Union. That is nearly six million Muslims in France today. They expect Muslims to make up between 12.7% to 18% by 2050, varying between scenarios going from zero migration to high migration. The 18% estimate is based on if immigration patterns of the last few years continue, which would mean there will be 13 million Muslims living in France by 2050. That is more than the entire population of Belgium.

This increase of Muslims in France leads to not only a demographic change in the country but also a cultural and religious change.

France has a long history. That history is interwoven with its Catholic faith. That interwoven history has resulted in many churches all over France. Now, thousands of churches are waiting for their destruction. The government has calculated that it is cheaper to demolish centuries-old buildings than renovate them. Thus, in comes the wrecking ball[76].

Currently, there are around 2500 mosques in France, but the construction of new mosques can hardly keep up with the demand. Supported by foreign funds from Morocco, Saudi Arabia and Algeria, new mosques are constantly being built. As Christianity and churches wither away, Islam and the new mosques grow. The future of France could not be any clearer or any more visible than by watching the cities change shape. In the France of the future, if current trends continue, it will not be the church

[75] Europe's Growing Muslim Population. 2018. [http://www.clovisinstitute.org/europes-growing-muslim-population/] (Accessed 11.07.22)

[76] FRANCE: 2800 Churches to be demolished, 1868 Neo Gothic Église Saint Jacques d'Abbeville, [MIRROR] 2016. The Internet Archive. [https://archive.org/details/youtube-6zq5d-I5D5M] (Accessed 11.07.22)

bells that wake people in the morning; it will be the calls for prayer coming from the mosque. In such a reality, it would not be difficult to imagine Notre Dame being replaced in importance and relevance by the Grand Mosque.

This is (to say the least) ironic, considering that the invading armies of the Islamic Caliphate in the battle of Poitiers in 732, where the French King Charles Martel defeated the Muslims and halted the Islamic invasion of Europe. Realistically, if it was not for the Franks' victory, no force in Europe could have stopped a further invasion of the Muslims. The Caliphate might have taken all of Europe if Charles Martel had lost the battle that day. Needless to say, this development is a stab back at the ancestors of France.

The Future Growth

Going back to the demographic situation, France has a relatively high fertility rate, and there are four babies born to every immigrant entering the country. This makes France look relatively healthy at first, but we have to take into consideration that 20% of France already consists of immigrants and their children. Moreover, since France's immigration has been taking place at a high pace since the end of World War 2 and the era of decolonization, there are third-generation immigrants that do not show up in those statistics. In other words, many of the 800.000 babies born will be of non-French descent. How many exactly is very hard to say. We know that the Muslim fertility rate in France is 2.9, versus a non-Muslim rate of 1.9. Consequently, the size of the Muslim group in France will multiply even without immigration. Further immigration will contribute to population growth, and immigration will mostly come from Islamic areas of Africa. Even with zero migration, France is expected to have Muslims making up over 12% of its population in three decades. If migration continues, this will be 18%. That means it will be 1 in 8 to nearly 1 in 5 who are Muslim. And if we take the whole non-white population, including non-Muslims, into consideration, the figure would of course, be even higher.

The latest numbers from France show that immigrants and descendants of non-European immigrants represent 3% of the age group 80+ years and

30% in the age group of 0-4 years. That is a 10 fold increase, and a statistical proof that there is a population replacement in France[77].

Conclusion

This means that the French population will slowly shrink over the long run and eventually reach a minority status if present trends continue. Exactly what year this turning point will happen is of less importance. It is also difficult to pinpoint, considering the lack of statistics available on this subject. The main point to highlight here is the demographic trend that the native French population is slowly being replaced.

This is a situation and development that the people of France do not want. Already, 47% of France agrees with the statement: "There are so many foreigners living here that it doesn't feel like home anymore"[78]. A stunning 75% say that France and Islam are not compatible, and 70% say there are too many foreigners in France already[79].

So, when will the French rekindle the Bastille fighting spirit?

14.4 From Glory to Despair - Italy

Italy is one of the oldest civilised territories on the European continent. In the distant past, Rome dominated Europe. Its cities flourished and were full of life.

Nowadays, Italy's villages are drained[80]. The young move into the cities or seek a brighter future abroad. The few that stay simply don't have enough

---

[77] La diversité des origines et la mixité des unions progressent au fil des générations. 2022. [https://www.insee.fr/fr/statistiques/6468640#figure2_radio1] (Accessed 16.08.22)

[78] Do Europeans feel at home in their country? 2018 CLOVIS INSTITUTE. [http://www.clovisinstitute.org/europeans-at-home/] (Accessed 11.07.22)

[79] 'Too many foreigners in France', French people say. 2013. [https://www.thelocal.fr/20130125/too-many-foreigners-in-france-french-say/] (Accessed 11.07.22)

[80] Who Will Save These Dying Italian Towns? 2017. [https://www.nytimes.com/2017/09/07/t-magazine/abandoned-italian-towns.html] (Accessed 11.07.22)

children to maintain the population. The Mayor of one of these small towns, Domenico Lucano, found an interesting solution to this depopulation problem. His village, Riace, invited migrants to rejuvenate the town. Currently, about a quarter of the two thousand inhabitants are migrants, primarily from Africa and Asia. The native Italians that still live there are mostly the elderly. The Guardian states the town has "secured its own future"[81].

Although most easily visible in the small villages, it is a trend taking place on the national level.

Italy's Population

To understand change, we must first understand the present. Italy has a population of just over 60 million, which has been fairly stable over the last decade. Since 2015, Italy's population has been shrinking slightly in recent years. That stability in population size is due to immigrants filling in the gaps. Italy's fertility rate is far below the replacement rate of 2.1, now at 1.37. The population has an average age of 44.9 years, and nearly one in four Italians is over 65[82]. Japan is the only country in the world with a higher percentage of 65 or older[83].

For comparison, Italy's prior colony, Ethiopia, has an average age of 17.6 years[84]. Although Ethiopia's fertility rate has decreased as well, it is still

[81] Kington, Tom. 2013. The tiny Italian village that opened its doors to migrants who braved the sea. [https://www.theguardian.com/world/2013/oct/12/italian-village-migrants-sea] (Accessed 11.07.22)

[82] Reuters Staff. 2017. Births in Italy hit record low in 2016, population ages. [https://www.reuters.com/article/us-italy-birthrate/births-in-italy-hit-record-low-in-2016-population-ages-idUSKBN16D28U] (Accessed 11.07.22)

[83] Romei, Valentina. 2017. Italian emigration continues despite strong economic recovery. The Financial Times Ltd. [https://www.ft.com/content/cb9bd2ee-c07d-11e7-9836-b25f8adaa111] (Accessed 11.07.22)

[84] Smith Oliver. 2017. Mapped: The world's most elderly (and youngest) countries. Telegraph Media Group Limited [https://www.telegraph.co.uk/travel/maps-and-graphics/oldest-and-youngest-countries-populations/] (Accessed 11.07.22)

sitting at a massive 4.6 children per woman. Enough to double the size of the next generation[85].

Rather than doubling its population size, Italy's fertility rate results in every generation being a third smaller than the last. Every new generation will be 30% smaller than the previous. A generation of 10 million Italians today will have 6.85 million children. They will have 4.7 million grandchildren and just over 3 million great-grandchildren. With a fertility rate of 1.37, 10 million has turned into 3 million within four generations.

Italy has not seen such a decline in its population since the Black Plague ravaged its lands. The only difference is that this time, rather than people dying, they were never born in the first place.

The Emigrants

There are 5.4 million Italians living abroad, over 1.5 million of which have moved abroad since the economic crisis of 2008. The total now represents nearly 10% of the total inhabitants of Italy and a disproportionate amount of young people. Despite recent growth in the Italian economy, its relatively high unemployment is pushing away the young and desperate. The unemployment rate in Italy sits at 10.8%, with youth unemployment above 30%.

Easy migration within the EU has led many Italians to seek a brighter and more prosperous future abroad. The elderly are the ones that remain.

In a country already out of balance due to the lack of babies being born, emigration further contributes to the population decline.

---

[85] Why Ethiopian women are having fewer children than their mothers. 2015. BBC. [https://www.bbc.com/news/world-africa-34732609] (Accessed 11.07.22)

In 2002, the total number of foreign nationals living in Italy numbered over 1 million. Since 2015 there have been over 5 million foreign nationals[86], approaching 10% of the total population. Foreign nationals exclude those that acquired Italian citizenship, as well as illegal immigrants. It is worth noting that half of the foreign nationals come from other European countries, notably Romania. Around half of the Europeans are from non-EU countries like Albania and Ukraine. The other half come primarily from Africa and Asia[87].

The inflow of non-EU citizens into Italy in 2016 alone amounted to 226.000. Most of these came as family reunification (45%), with the second most prominent reason being humanitarian reasons and asylum (34%). Only 5.8% gave the reason for work to move to Italy[88].

Out of the foreign nationals, 185.000 acquired Italian citizenship in 2016 and thereby ceased to belong to the category of foreign nationals. From then onward, they will be counted as part of the regular Italian population. The 185.000 consisted primarily of Moroccans and Albanians, as well as significant numbers of Indians, Bangladeshi and Pakistani.

---

[86] Ricostruzione della popolazione residente per etá, sess e cittadinanza nei comuni. 2011. Istat – Istituto nazionale di statistica. [https://www.istat.it/it/archivio/99464] (Accessed 11.07.22)

[87] Non-EU citizens: presence, new inflows and acquisition of citizenship. 2017. Istat – Istituto nazionale di statistica. [https://www.istat.it/en/archive/204320] (Accessed 11.07.22)

[88] Non-EU Citizens. Years 2016-2017. Istat – Istituto nazionale di statistica. [https://www.istat.it/en/files/2017/10/Infographic-Non-EU-citizens-in-Italy.-Years-2016-2017.pdf] (Accessed 11.07.22)

The Illegal Immigrants

Before the start of the migrant crisis, there were already an estimated 670.000 illegal immigrants in Italy back in 2008[89]. In 2016 alone, a total of 180.000 illegal migrants reached the Italian coast from Libya; the number that is present in Italy might have remained fairly constant as most continued their paths to Germany and Sweden. Removing half a million illegal immigrants is still a hot topic in Italian politics[90].

In 2017, the Italian coastguard seized an NGO vessel operated by a German organisation, claiming it was aiding illegal migration from the Libyan coast to Italy[91]. Yet, simultaneously, the Italian government decided to bypass the Mediterranean Sea and promised to bring 10.000 Libyans to Rome by plane[92].

Islam in Italy

Currently, 4.8% of Italians are Muslim, close to three million. According to Pew Research, this will be between 8% and 14% by 2050[93]. The range varies from 8% with zero migration to 14% with a high migration scenario, as we have seen over the last several years. However, these numbers exclude illegal immigrants whose religious leaning is unknown. Despite being

[89] Rosenthal, Elisabeth. 2008. Italy cracks down on illegal immigration. NY Times Co. [http://archive.boston.com/news/world/europe/articles/2008/05/16/italy_cracks_down_on_illegal_immigration/] (Accessed 11.07.22)

[90] Nick Squires. 2018. Italian politician pledges to kick out half a million illegal migrants if elected prime minister. Telegraph Media Group Limited. [https://www.telegraph.co.uk/news/2018/01/23/italian-politician-pledges-kick-half-million-illegal-migrants/] (Accessed 11.07.22)

[91] Pantaleone, Wladimiro. 2017. Italy seizes NGO rescue boat for allegedly aiding illegal migration. Reuters. [https://www.reuters.com/article/us-europe-migrants-italy-ngo/italy-seizes-ngo-rescue-boat-for-allegedly-aiding-illegal-migration-idUSKBN1AI21B] (Accessed 11.07.22)

[92] Kington, Tom. 2017. Italy vows to bring in 10,000 migrants from Libya by plane. Times Newspapers Ltd [https://www.thetimes.co.uk/article/italy-vows-to-bring-in-10-000-migrants-from-libya-by-plane-9jpj5vjzw] (Accessed 11.07.22)

[93] Europe's Growing Muslim Population. 2018. [http://www.clovisinstitute.org/europes-growing-muslim-population/] (Accessed 11.07.22)

unknown, one could make an educated guess based on the countries of origin and conclude that a large percentage of the illegal immigrants is Muslim.

Although southern Italy was temporarily under the control of the Caliphate, the Norman invasion of Sicily ended the Islamic era. The Muslims either fled or converted to Christianity. The renewed presence of Islam in Italy, the home of the Catholic Church, started in the last century with Somalians arriving. The current presence of Islam is purely due to the migrants arriving from Islamic countries.

Births and deaths

Total births in 2016 amounted to 474.000, while deaths in the same year totalled 608.000. A difference of 134.000. The total population decreased by 86.000. The difference between the 134.000 and the 86.000 can be explained by net migration. With 115.000 Italians moving abroad in the same year, a simple calculation can show us the total immigration. Total loss was 608.000 (deaths) plus 115.000 (emigration), a total of 723.000. The total gains were 723.000 minus the shrinkage of 86.000, bringing us to 637.000. Out of these, 637.000 births accounted for 474.000. That leaves 163.000 immigrants to supplement the population.

This number of 163.000 roughly matches the number given above. You will find that when it comes to these statistics on immigration, different sources often quote slightly different numbers, yet always in the same direction.

Our calculation shows that a quarter of population replacement currently comes from immigration. However, many of the births will also be from non-Italian parents, as they have, on average, younger age and higher fertility rate.

The Future of Italy

We mentioned above that the generations are shrinking. With fertility of 1.37, the 474.000 babies born last year will only create 325.000 children and 222.000 grandchildren. But here comes the one worth remembering;

they will only have around 150.000 great-grandchildren. If current fertility continues, which so far has been rather constant, and migration continues in a similar trend, then within four generations. In that case, the majority of new Italians will not be Italian babies being born but migrants coming into the country.

In the scenario above, it will mean that Italians will turn into a minority in their own country from that point onward. As a generation lasts around twenty-five years, we will reach this turning point within a century.

Which babies are Italian?

However, we have missed out on one thing in our calculation. Those 474.000 babies are not all Italian. Ten percent of the country is a foreign nation, which would leave roughly 426.000 babies born to Italian nationals. They would have only 200.000 grandchildren and 137.000 great-grandchildren.

But, that is not all. Of these Italian nationals, many will have a migration background. Unfortunately, such numbers are not tracked, and we would have to guess. Nonetheless, the foreign nationals will account for 22.000 grandchildren and 15.000 great-grandchildren, assuming their fertility rate is the same as that of the average Italian. That is a wild and improbable assumption, so 22.000 would be a rather low estimate.

Which babies are Muslim?

Now, remember that 4.8% of Italy is Muslim. Across Europe, the average fertility rate for Muslims is 2.6 as opposed to the Italian 1.37. First, this would mean Muslims are over-represented compared to their 4.8% in the 474.000 births, as Muslim women are more likely to have children. For the sake of simplicity, let us assume 5% of the births are Muslim. A low estimate. That makes 23700 births Muslim. Keep in mind that the number of Muslim births overlaps with the births of foreign nationals. Because the Muslims have a fertility rate higher than the replacement rate, these 23.700 Muslims will have 40.000 grandchildren and 52.000 great-grandchildren.

The Results

Thus, within four generations, we will see 137.000 babies of Italian national ancestry. We will see 22.000 babies of foreign national ancestry. And out of this total of 150.000, one in three will be Muslim with ancestors living in Italy today.

- These are the babies born in a ZERO migration scenario.
- It excludes all babies born from immigrants yet to arrive in Italy.
- It excludes babies from illegal immigrants.
- It includes babies from Italian nationals with a migration background.

Adding in all the factors for which the data is unavailable, or the computations go beyond our capability, would lead to more exact and shocking results.

Only 222.000 grandchildren will be born to the children in 2016; out of these, 40.000 Muslim are babies born in Italy from its current Muslim population. Moreover, yearly immigration adds 160.000 newcomers a year. Already the non-Islamic Italian nationals' grandchildren of the generation born today will form a minority part of the population growth of Italy. Since a generation is generally calculated as twenty-five years, the grandchildren we are speaking of are a mere fifty years from now. The scenario we described is the scenario of 2070.

Italians may maintain the majority for a while longer, but its dominance will be in the 65+ category, rather than in the youth and middle-aged that control the nation. Italians will become strangers in their own country.

However, there is a new wind blowing over Europe. We see the same trend in Italy as in Sweden. In the recent 2022 parliament election a national concervative coalition won a resounding victory in Italy. The political party Brothers of Italy became the largest party in the country, receiving about 26% of the votes. The Brothers of Italy are newcomers to the national political scene in Italy, and have enjoyed rapid growth and success under the leadership of its charismatic leader Giorgia Meloni, who will also become Italy's first female prime minister. Together with Berlusconi's Forza Italia and Salvini's Lega, the Brothers of Italy is now at the forefront of the new governing coalition in the country. This coalition can be described as conservative centre-right with a mix of populist elements. Together the three parties received 43.7% and 44% of the votes in the Lower House and the Upper House respectively. It is interesting to note that the populist party the Five Star Movement, that claims to neither be on the right or the left, also received about 15,5% in both chambers of parliament. The Five Star Movement is in many respects a partner that the new governing coalition can and should be able to cooperate with. In total, the populist and conservative right parties in Italy received about 60% of the votes[94].

[94] 2022. Estimated percentage of votes won in the chamber of deputies and senate in the Italian general election of 2022, by coalition. Statista. [https://www.statista.com/statistics/1335834/italy-election-results/] (Accessed 4.10.22)

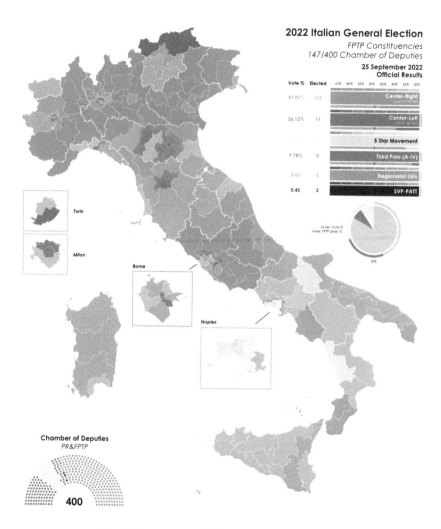

Ill. 10: Election map of the Italian 2022 election.[95]

Note: The blue areas show the districts where the Centre-Right coalition led by Ms. Meloni won a majority of representatives

[95] 2022 Italian general election. Wikimedia Foundation. [https://upload.wikimedia.org/wikipedia/commons/8/8d/2022_Italian_General_Election_Deputies_Single_Member_Seats.svg] (Accessed 4.10.22)

Especially Lega and the Brothers of Italy have fronted pro nativist and protectionist policies with emphasis on tradition, heritage and national identity. They have proposed tax cuts for families, tax cuts for small businesses and vowed to stop all illegal immigration, especially the immigration coming across the mediterranian from Africa and the Middle east. Giorgia Meloni has described herself as "Woman, Mother, Christian"[96], and contrasted this with the modern identity, or rather the non-identity, of global consumerism. Furthermore, she has pointed out what she calls "international financial speculators" as the culprits of Italy's dire situation with regards to their demographic and economic situation. It is apparent that the Italian people were hungry for this. In a poll from 2018, 52% of Italians agree with the statement "There are so many foreigners here that it does not feel like home anymore"[97]. And this sentiment was expressed very clearly in the 2022 election in Italy.

It stands to reason to expect that more countries in Europe will follow this trend that we are observing in countries such as Poland, Hungary, and now more recently in Sweden and Italy, as the demographic crisis becomes more and more apparent. This combined with the economic downturn we are now experiencing will cause reactions to the liberal globalist policies all over Europe in the coming years. It will be interesting to keep a close eye on the development in Europe's two major countries; Germany and France. Especially in France, since they have a long standing and well developed conservative patriotic opposition to the current ruling liberal elite. Judging by the Yellow Vests protests in France going on from november 2018 until the present, change is bound to come. If this change will be for the better or the worse, only time will tell. What is certain is that the current situation is not tenable, nor sustainable.

---

[96] 2022. 'Woman, mother, Christian' guides Italian far-right to brink of power. Euractiv. [https://www.euractiv.com/section/elections/news/woman-mother-christian-guides-italian-far-right-to-brink-of-power/] (Accessed 4.10.22)

[97] Do Europeans feel at home in their country? 2018 CLOVIS INSTITUTE. [http://www.clovisinstitute.org/europeans-at-home/] (Accessed 11.07.22)

15. Is The Great Replacement a genocide?

This article is based on a translation from a podcast[98] by Martin Sellner on Dec 4, 2019.

I believe we have come to a point where anyone knows that the great replacement is a reality and that it corresponds to the most significant demographic change in the structure of our population.

Some deny it for tactical and political reasons, some others judge it differently or do not perceive it as not so tragic and do not weigh its political consequences, but no one can deny that this great replacement is happening.

I would like to discuss whether this phenomenon we observe is the definition of genocide[99]. On December the 9th, 1948, the UN decided on a convention on the prevention and punishment of the crime of genocide. In the second article, the term genocide is defined at length and at one point states: "Intentionally imposing on the group conditions of life likely to bring about its physical destruction in whole or in part." The question now is how conditions of life are defined, which can be found in a document of the Human Rights Commission of the UN from the 17th of April 1998 concerning the Declaration on Population Transfers and the Sedentary Detention of Settlers, in which unlawful politics are being described. Article 6 of this decision is stated: "Any practice or policy that has the purpose or effect of changing the demographic composition of a region in which a national, ethnic, linguistic or other minority or indigenous population resides, whether by displacement, resettlement and/or by settling settlers, or any combination thereof, is unlawful."

Let us ask ourselves objectively if, according to this definition, unlawful conduct applies here. According to the first part of this article ("Any

---

[98] Entlarvt: Ist der Bevölkerungsaustausch ein Völkermord? - Mirror Martin Sellner. 2019. altCensored.com. [https://www.altcensored.com/watch?v=R1ZImZv175I] (Accessed 11.07.22)

[99] The Genocide Convention. United Nations. [https://www.un.org/en/genocideprevention/genocide-convention.shtml] (Accessed 11.07.22)

practice or policy that has the purpose or effect of changing the demographic composition of a region"), the great replacement applies here since it is practically as well as in the orientation of the migration policy, which points towards a sustainable and unchangeable ethnic recomposition of the regions and the countries. This is presented to us as our future, as shown by the Deutsche Welle, which states: "Herbert Brücker, who heads the migration research department at the Federal Institute for Employment Research (IAB), told the Welt daily on Monday that Germany "will become more diverse."

"Currently, about a quarter of the people in Germany have a migrant background," Brücker said. "In 20 years, it will be at least 35%, but could also be more than 40%."

He noted that in cities, that figure is likely to be higher. "What we see in the big cities today will be normal for the country as a whole in the future," Brücker said. "In a city like Frankfurt, we'll have between 65% to 70%."[100]

Now, the second part of the paragraph states who would be subject to it: "a region in which a national, ethnic, linguistic or other minority or indigenous population resides". It is yet crystal-clear that we Europeans are indigenous, autochtone people in this region and that we thus have the right to maintain our existence on this continent.

The third part of this paragraph mentions "displacement, resettlement and/or by settling settlers, or any combination thereof", and applies evidently to the phenomenon described here since we are discussing the transfer of massive parts of the population to another region, changing thus the very structure of the local population.

The question of whether or not the situation happening now is a mathematically proven replacement of the population can thus, following the very definition of the United Nations itself, be augmented. This policy is not only unlawful, but it eventually is an actual genocide. I believe the

---

[100] 2019. Germany: In 20 years, 1 in 3 people will have migrant roots. Deutsche Welle. [https://www.dw.com/en/germany-in-20-years-1-in-3-people-will-have-migrant-roots/a-51101172] (Accessed 11.07.22)

question is no longer whether or not we are witnessing a great replacement of our population but whether or not we are still living in a democracy: has the population been advised on what phenomenon was being implemented? Were the consequences of this policy explained? Were the population asked whether or not they did agree with the definitive change of their demographic structure?

I demand hereby that the German government cease any policy that may result in the destruction of German culture, such as the planned settlement of non-Europeans in large numbers to push back the German population, and the persecution of the representatives of German culture.

16. What will happen?

The Stock market

We can expect a declining stock market soon. Large pension funds are keeping the world's stock markets under control.

Richard Mahoney of the Centre for the Study of American Business states that more than two-thirds of all listed US stocks are in retirement accounts[101].

Who will buy all these stocks when one of every three adults is over 65?

Europe's retirement system is collapsing. European politicians have "stolen" most of the money and spent it on other projects, and the coming generation of productive workers is not large enough to support the increasing pension claims from the ageing population. Their stock markets are too small to buy the American pension funds shares when the American shareholders retire and want to cash out their investments.

According to Thornton Parker, in his internet article "Boomers' Time Bomb", written November 16, 1998, the American stocks-for-retirement-cycle has a fatal flaw.

The value of all US stocks is about half the total of the world's stock markets. Asia is no longer the economic powerhouse it once was, Parker says. What remains is India and Africa. India has to shoulder the big burden of the future stock market, as there are no prospects from Africa to do so.

We see that the American pension system is hazardous and could be compared to a pyramid scam.

The hope is a vital and flourishing India. Still, it would take enormous changes to turn India into a competitive society, changes that perhaps would cause India to see a lower birth rate.

---

[101] Parker, Thornton. 1998. Boomers' Time Bomb. [https://www.barrons.com/articles/SB911013381436194000] Dow Jones & Company, Inc. (Accessed 11.07.22)

This produces additional guarantees of pension payments because the biggest part of the investment policy will consist of personal savings accumulated in a commercial pension fund. The increasing share of these funds in a pension system makes up for the lack of government support for sufficient pension payments for older people at the expense of the incomes of working people. This happens in a situation with inadequate demographic balance.

The necessity for reforms is supported by the results of sociological surveys made in European countries and in the US. This research shows declining trust in state pension guarantees. It is especially noticeable among the young generation.

The country's economy and especially the stock market are greatly influenced by the status of the pension system and the share of private pension funds in it. Nowadays, pension funds make up a significant percentage of the stock market. The political and economic future of Western countries depends on their growth.

The pension system crisis

The existing mechanism of pension provision will not be viable when the amount of pensioners increases and the amount of young working people paying money into the pension system declines. In most Western countries, pension systems are based on a pretty simple scheme: Working members of society support pensioners, counting on the fact that their pensions will be provided with payments from the next generation.

Nowadays, the pension system resembles a classic financial pyramid scam, being based on the constant replenishment of funds from new players. Modern demographic tendencies can lead to the collapse of the existing state social guarantees and the collapse of the pension pyramid. The pyramid type of pension system cannot adjust to the new demographic explosions and, therefore, must be reformed.

A more straightforward, less realistic solution is to increase the amount of money working people give to the pension system or cut down on state support of retirees. But these actions can cause more social problems.

Therefore, we should look at the other model of pension provision created mainly in Anglo-Saxon countries. The role of non-governmental pension funds in Great Britain, The Netherlands and the US is more significant than that held by traditional north European pension systems.

Pension fund assets as a percentage of GNP

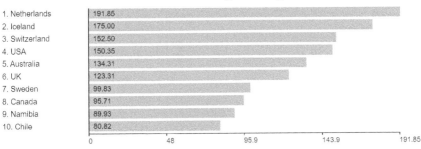

1. Netherlands	191.85
2. Iceland	175.00
3. Switzerland	152.50
4. USA	150.35
5. Australia	134.31
6. UK	123.31
7. Sweden	99.83
8. Canada	95.71
9. Namibia	89.93
10. Chile	80.82

Table 9: Pension fund assets as a percentage of GNP[102]

Note: Definition: Ratio of assets of pension funds to GDP. A pension fund is any plan, fund, or scheme that provides retirement income. Data taken from a variety of sources such as OECD, AIOS, FIAP and national sources.

The Future health care system

The populations of Europe, Japan and North America are getting noticeably older each year. Soon, the average age in Europe[103] and the US will be almost 50 (for comparison: the average age of an American resident in 1850 was 19 years).

High birth rates in developed countries in the 1950s and the beginning of the 1960s (the "baby boom") have influenced future demographic indices. Today, people of the baby-boom generation are becoming pensioners. The number of older people will exceed the amount of young for the first time in the history of civilised countries. But low birth rates

---

[102] Ratio of assets of pension funds to GDP [https://www.theglobaleconomy.com/rankings/pension_funds_assets/G7/] (Accessed 11.07.22)

[103] eurostat Statistics Explained. 2020. [https://ec.europa.eu/eurostat/statistics-explained/index.php?title=Ageing_Europe_-_statistics_on_population_developments] (Accessed 11.07.22)

have also created this situation. Life expectancy has risen steadily worldwide over the last few decades, especially in developed countries.

Europe and Japan will face a disaster in the future. Their governments are not prepared to deal with this catastrophe. They are too caught up in day-to-day problems and cannot extend their outlook to include long-term concerns. Old Europe started to import foreigners to take care of the old Europeans, but with little to no success, combined with the high social costs associated with immigration. To integrate persons from other cultures, one needs skills, experience and strict guidelines, which are wholly lacking under the current immigration regime.

It is obvious that in the future, there will not be enough human resources in Old Europe and Japan and that health care in these countries will become extremely expensive. People now 40 - 50 years old will face inhumane medical treatment and pay hilariously high prices for services they already paid through their taxes.

With this development, we now risk that Old Europe will gather its elderly and put them crammed together in particular institutions or let them die alone at home — the least expensive option.

Life expectancies 1900 - 2019

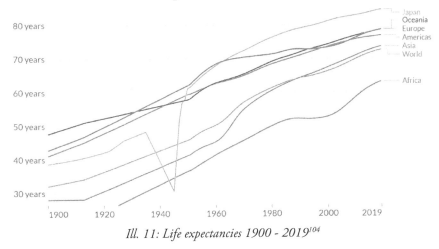

Ill. 11: Life expectancies 1900 - 2019[104]

Modern medicine and medical technology make it possible to preserve health well into old age. Due to low birth rates and the rise in life expectancy, the amount of old-age "baby boomers" will exceed the younger generation in the coming decades. Demographic processes in highly developed countries will change the way of life in all spheres.

Earlier, society was primarily oriented toward young people. Soon the prevalence of older people will lead to size able changes in the economy, politics, and even personal relations.

Social effects: Old Europe will explode

Due to the depopulation of native Europeans and increased immigration, Old Europe will erupt into internal conflicts.

Continued immigration will increase cultural conflicts in Old Europe and slowly but surely build up tension that will lead to chaos and potentially a disastrous civil confrontation. All the different cultures thriving in the Western Hemisphere today will struggle for a change in their favour when the liberal regime can no longer provide effective governance.

---

[104] Life expectancies 1900 - 2019 [https://ourworldindata.org/life-expectancy] (Accessed 11.07.22)

125

This will happen because liberal women do not produce the required number of children to compete with the foreign cultures in Old Europe and their homelands.

These foreign cultures will never accept the liberal ideas of the West because they realise that the liberal concept has no future.

They are looking at life from a long-term perspective to support their traditions and religions. Western liberal cultures do not have this long-term perspective and will, under these circumstances, lose out.

What will happen in the Western world?

The stronger alien cultures will never let their own culture die out, and they will demand places to maintain their traditions and worship their religion inside western countries.

The liberal horizon is 4-6 years. Foreign traditional cultures, and the totalitarian state system in China, seem to look many generations ahead; therefore, they have survived and will survive into the future. Traditional western culture also has this quality of long-term perspective, and that is why it is so important to reconnect with our traditions and traditional way of thinking.

When the powerful foreign cultures become strong enough inside our western countries, and the followers of liberal values become a minority, hot conflict and potentially civil war will start among the different factions. A liberal regime cannot survive in such conditions, and the only way for western countries and identities to be protected and stay is for the West to assert its authority and turn towards a more traditional form of government; to rekindle the formula that once made the West rise to the top.

End of democracy in Old Europe

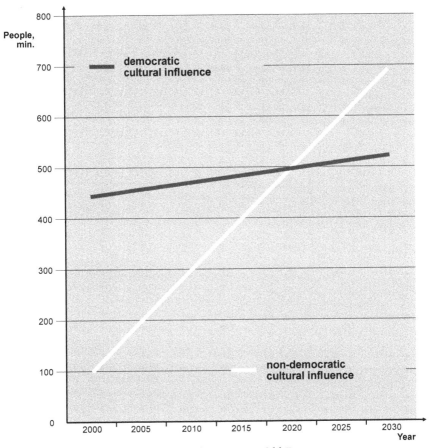

Ill. 12: End of democracy in Old Europe

Note: This graph is calculated based on Professor Alexander Tytler's "200-year circle" and the increase of non-democratic cultures in Europe, according to country statistics on births, deaths and migration.

Women voting rights wil disappear in Old Europe

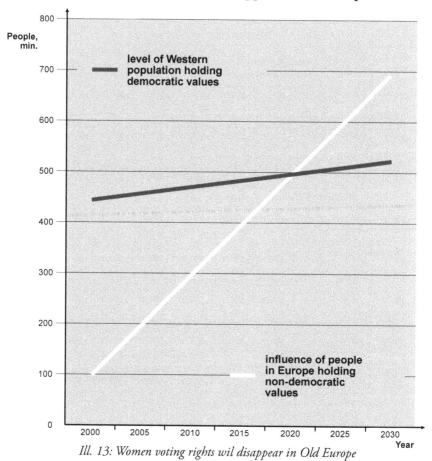

Ill. 13: Women voting rights wil disappear in Old Europe

Note: This graph is based on demographic statistics from the Population Reference Bureau and Tytler's "200-year circle".

Therefore the culture that must rise to power in Europe will be male-dominated, regarding female influence in politics as dangerous, and imposing restrictions on their right to vote.

Something like this is only probable if a civil war in Old Europe will upend the liberal order as we know it today.

No more free press in Old Europe

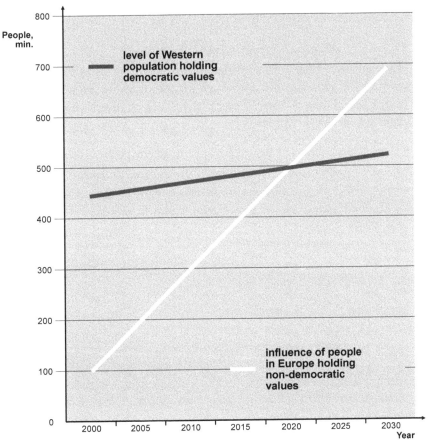

Ill. 14: No more free press in Old Europe

Note: This graph is based on European country statistics and intertwined with chaos theory.

No more free press

The "political correctness" preventing the discussion of increasing degeneracy, complacency and the coming cultural and ethnic conflict in Europe will cause the downfall of the free press.

The press in Old Europe could not debate cultural or long-term problems due to its ideological blindness. There is a liberal elite view that is dominating and killing all other opinions that are not "politically correct".

This "political correctness" comes from the liberal illusions currently so pervasive in Western culture, which tends to "block" free debate and free thought. Quite ironically, the established press and the liberal political order are undermining their continued existence by cutting off their lifeblood through this "political correctness".

We already see editors censoring many articles that attempt to debate immigration questions. By advocating for the freedom of certain non-democratic religions and cultures, politicians and policymakers will cause the death of the free press and their liberal regime in Europe.

These European politicians and policymakers are responsible for what will happen to themselves in the future for blindly promoting this political correctness and replacing their etnic population.

In response to the increasing tension between non-democratic and democratic cultures in Europe and the world, America and Europe have developed technology to control the population, such as electronic mass surveillance, centralisation of authority and getting rid of cash. This move towards a totalitarian solution to the mounting problems in the west is, in fact, a step away from a traditional long-term solution to our demographic and economic issues. A solution with which to preserve western liberty within a tradition is to 1) reduce the ethnic tension in western nations by repatriating foreign immigrants, 2) promote policies that will increase the birth rate by investing in the future of one's people, 3) sustainable long term monetary policy NOT based on credit or debt, leading to over taxation and 4) balance between the sizes of the financial and production sectors in the economy.

Conflict and a new beginning in Old Europe

According to our model of chaos, the ordered structure of modern Western society will break down and must take another form. As we know, democracy is a very fragile construction and does not tend to last for a long time. There will be forces struggling to implement their will under the mantle of law and order, but they will not be democratic.

As we mentioned earlier, when the Finnish philosopher Georg Henrik von Wright asked Professor Ludwig Wittgenstein in 1936 if there would be a war in Europe, Wittgenstein answered, "There will be two or three."

Just look at the prolonged conflict in Northern Ireland between two Christian groups and other subgroups. Just imagine what will happen when you have more significant numbers of opposite groups facing nose to nose. The conflict will be long and bloody. Old Europe does not have the economic power to engage and integrate the opposing cultural forces. Attempts to do so will only cost more and more.

A Swedish Professor of Macroeconomics at the University of Växjö, Mr Bo Södersten, and a Professor of Macroeconomics at the International Business School at Jönkoping, Mr Mats Hammarstedt, together with Mr Dan-Olof Rooth, a PhD in Macroeconomics at the University of Kalmar, argue that the failure to assimilate immigrants costs Sweden about 2% of GNP per year or US$3 billion.

Without successful assimilation, immigration will only create cultural conflict. Why should Old Europe be spared if all other democracies and complex late-stage cultures have been crushed due to their impertinence and complacency? There is no reason to believe that liberal Europe will become a historical exception. We see lawlessness, terrorism and social unrest spreading through most European countries. The number of burglaries, murders, rapes, and domestic violence is increasing. Pension systems are breaking down. Drug and alcohol consumption is rising.

Only a rebirth of Europe in the flames of its traditions can save the continued existence of the European peoples and their transhistorical identities.

Remember, you are responsible

You are responsible for doing your part, but what can you do?

Here are some suggestions for concrete actions that you can take:

1. Make more children! At least 3 per couple.

2. Talk to everybody, your family, friends and colleagues about this demography topic.

3. Demand money from the government to support your family so you can afford more children.

4. Demand kindergarten and educational support for each child.

5. Pay grandparents in an intelligent way to take care of their grandchildren while parents may be busy with work.

6. Found at least one demographic institute that is not controlled and directed by globalist interests.

7. The prime minister or president of each country should at least have 3 children to be an example for their country.

8. Introduce a no-child tax — a carrot-and-stick approach.

9. Do not read mainstream media. Find alternative press on; Bitchute, Odysee, Rumble, Gab, Gateway Pundit, Breitbart, X22 report, Dr Steve Turley and so on.

10. Talk to people in your community about these issues when you meet them in your everyday life.

11. Set goals. For example, The Norwegian population will be 10 million Norwegians born in Norway.

12. Be happy; believe that significant change for the better is possible and will come when the free people of Europe wake up.

There will be enormous changes in European society no matter how the future plays out. And we can change it for the better! If you act now! We have an historical opportunity now that the petrodollar will be phased out and the gold-link currencies are moving to take over. The BRICS countries will strengthen their position going forward. This will mark a shift in geopolitical power away from liberal globalist power centres. This will create an opening for new policies and new political constellations, even here in the West. And this will hopefully awaken more people.

Open your eyes, think for yourself and focus on your family and local community. Talk to your neighbours and bond with those closest to you rather than to spend your energy on chasing illusory prestige in globalistic institutions and media. Turn off your TV, turn off the radio. Be happy, nourish your family life and make more children!

There is no overpopulation in the West. You are being fooled. It is the other way around!

Be proud of yourself and your kinsmen. Take to the streets when the time comes and demand your rights.

About Legatum Publishing

Legatum Publishing strives to produce books and related material with wholesome content for students, parents and children.

It has been said that history is a pact between the dead, the living and the yet unborn. We believe this statement to be true; it is the goal of Legatum Publishing to offer books that will help Europeans and people of European ancestry discover more about their unique history and develop an appreciation for the legacy that they have inherited.

We want to assist parents in granting knowledge to the next generation by providing them with interesting books - including some older titles that are becoming increasingly forgotten or neglected in the modern world.

Other publications
by Legatum Publishing

The Sieges of Vienna by the Turks

In his 1845 work The Sieges of Vienna by the Turks, the Austrian topographer, cultural historian and writer Karl August Schimmer elegantly describes the events of the Siege of Vienna (1529) and Battle of Vienna (1683).

Schimmer identifies how, in both instances, a coalition of European troops fought side by side in order to save Vienna and all of Europe from Ottoman invasion. In 1529 Bohemians, Spaniards and Portuguese were all represented among the city's defenders, and the siege of 1683 saw the famous intervention of King Jan Sobieski's Polish Winged Hussars to prevent Ottoman advancement into Europe.

Schimmer had a goal of promoting patriotism through a colourful writing style. It is our strong belief the book was written to a high scholarly standard. It succeeds in conveying a wide range of information regarding the two wars, especially in contextualising the background that led to the two famous battles, while remaining accessible and engaging to the reader.

For this reason we believe that The Sieges of Vienna by the Turks is an important book for the celebration of our common European history and identity.

Legatum Publishing AS are proud to present this updated reprint, which includes a new foreword, illustrations and a short biography of Karl August Schimmer, giving contemporary readers the opportunity to immerse themselves in these historical events.

Karl August Schimmer

The Sieges of Vienna by the Turks

Defenders of the Golden Apple,

by Tore Rasmussen

"Defenders of the Golden Apple – An illustrated history book for kids about the battle of Vienna in 1683" is an educational book about the Battle of Vienna in 1683 for children aged 8-14. It tells the tale of the desperate struggle of the heroic defenders of Vienna against the invading Ottoman Empire. Lasting two months from July to September 1683, the siege brought the city to the brink of collapse.

Vienna, or the "Golden Apple" (its Ottoman nickname), was the jewel in the crown of Europe. The capture of this city would not only have been a military victory for the Ottomans, but a crushing spiritual defeat for Austria and all of Christendom.

This book is also a tale of hope and personal courage. It shows how different parts of Europe came together to unite against a common threat. This historical example gives hope that fraternity among the nations of Europe is possible in times of need.

In this story we find the virtues of bravery, personal responsibility and perseverance in the face of grave dangers and great difficulty. We have chosen a writing style for this book that is exciting and engaging for children to read and to listen to. Through this, we hope to stimulate their curiosity about history; to inspire them to read and explore for themselves.

This book is intended as a work of educational entertainment. While older children and teenagers can easily read it on their own, it is recommended that parents and tutors co-read this book together with the child to enhance their learning experience. The book comes with a complimentary glossary that explains new and difficult words that the child may not yet be familiar with.

DEFENDERS OF THE GOLDEN APPLE

Tore Rasmussen

Fridtjof Nansen: A Book for The Young

This is a contemporary account of Fridtjof Nansen's early life and endeavors. It takes us through Nansen's boyhood and formative years, all the way up to the famous North Pole expedition on his ship Fram. It is written in an engaging and accessible style for young people.

Fridtjof Nansen was one of the greatest polar explorers of the late 19th and early 20th century, and a folk hero to the Norwegian people. In 1896 he won international renown upon returning from his polar expedition. Soon afterwards in 1905 Nansen became a champion of Norwegian independence; he drew heavily on his prestige to secure international support for this cause. Towards the end of his life he became responsible for organizing humanitarian aid, contributing significantly towards saving millions of people from starvation in the 1920s.

This book focuses on the first half of Nansen's life up until his return from the polar expedition. It portrays the development of personal qualities and the trials of an extraordinary character.

We join Nansen on a journey of incredible hardships and overcoming insurmountable odds through diligence, determination, impeccable leadership and comradery. On his polar expeditions he and his crew faced lethal dangers many times as they braved the harsh elements of the far north. Fridtjof Nansen is an exemplar of the highest order and his deeds may serve as a source of inspiration for generations to come.

Author Jacob B. Bull, translated by Barnard, M. R. (Mordaunt Roger)

FRIDTJOF NANSEN
A BOOK FOR THE YOUNG

JACOB B. BULL

Vienna 1683, by Henry Elliot Malden

Henry Elliot Malden (1849-1931) was honorary secretary of the Royal Historical Society for 30 years and a fellow of the same Institution. In the preface to his book Vienna 1683, published in 1883, precisely 200 years after the Battle of Vienna, Malden writes: "The historical scholar will find nothing new in the following pages; but I have thought it worthwhile to tell to the general reader a story worth the telling and to explain not only the details, but the broader bearings also, of a great crisis in European history, no satisfactory account of which exists, I believe, in English, and the two hundredth anniversary of which is now upon us".

It is our firm belief that this book has greater relevance now than ever before. In a time of alarming historical illiteracy and rampant propaganda of the past, this entertaining and informative account of the events of the siege of Vienna will provide the reader with information and details that are no longer taught by schools and universities across the western world.

Legatum Publishing decided to reprint this book in 2021, including a new foreword, biography and illustrations. We do this to provide the modern reader with a valuable and concise tool to better understand the history and importance of 1683's Battle of Vienna, a vital episode in the history of our continent. "Historia Magistra vitae" (History is life's teacher) reads a famous Latin adage, which we hold to be true indeed. We must not forget our history, for, without history, there is no foundation for culture, and without this, there is no future.

138 years have passed since this excellent work was first published, and it is high time for it to receive a new edition. This is but one of many works risking fading into permanent obscurity, and as they pass out of recognition, so too fades a collective sense of our history and roots as Europeans. It is our firm hope that with the republishing of this work, we at Legatum Publishing will be making a contribution to the renewal of awareness and appreciation among Europeans for their history and identity and that it might help to counteract the efforts of those forces that seek to deny and diminish this, our European legacy.

HENRY ELLIOT MALDEN

VIENNA
1683

Four Figures of the German Conservative Revolution

Under the Weimar Republic, hundreds of authors, theoreticians and political personalities were part of the Conservative Revolution, named thus after 1945. This vast movement of thought and action, divided into multiple currents and tendencies, brought together those opponents of the Treaty of Versailles who refused to join the forming Nazism.

After 1933, under the Third Reich, they were mainly marginalized, doomed to "internal exile", and sometimes persecuted or forced into exile. Alain de Benoist presents in this book four emblematic figures of this movement: the economist Werner Sombart, a great specialist in the history of the social movement; Arthur Moeller van den Bruck, leader of the Berlin young conservatives, who was an implacable critic of liberal ideology, Ernst Niekisch, theoretician of National Bolshevism with an excellent itinerary (he was imprisoned both under the Weimar Republic and under National Socialism), and finally Oswald Spengler, the famous author of Decline of the West, whose harsh prophecies marked the century. Unrecognized for a long time, they deserve to be rediscovered today.

Alain de Benoist

Four Figures of the German Conservative Revolution

**Werner Sombart - Arthur Moeller van den Bruck
Ernst Niekisch - Oswald Spengler**

History and Tradition of the Europeans: 30 000 Years of Identity

This book was conceived from the questions of a historian witness of his time. It answers the questions the French ask themselves in a new spirit. What is France? What is Europe? What are we, and where are we going?

For Dominique Venner, Europe was not born of the Maastricht Treaty. Europe comes from a cultural community back to the most distant prehistory. It defines itself as a very ancient civilization, drawing its wealth from its constituent peoples, from the history and the spiritual heritage that has often had to be defended.

Returning to the sources is an object of this work which is intended to be a metaphysics of history. We will discover what we have in our own right from the Homeric poems, the Celtic and Nordic legends, the Roman heritage, the medieval imagination, courtly love... We will follow the quest for our authentic European tradition, a way to be unique in the face of life, death, love and destiny.

Dominique Venner was a writer and historian. He published over forty books, including Gettysburg, Critical History of the Resistance, History of Collaboration, The Whites and the Reds, and The Rebellious Heart. His work, "The History of the Red Army", was awarded by the French Academy. He was also editor of the Nouvelle Revue d'Histoire.

Dominique
VENNER

History and Tradition of the Europeans:

30 000 Years of Identity

LEGATUM
PUBLISHING
Identity · History · Knowledge

Legitimate Preference

This book brings together the observations and reasons that led the author to an unprecedented shift in opinion: preferring Europeans when one is European would be a spontaneous attitude, often totally unconscious. But saying so in public requires a solid prior reflection. Legitimising this attitude in such a way as to make it go viral requires more than clear arguments: it requires a clear overview of the advantages promised by a society where we could freely prefer our fellow Europeans. According to the author, our modern societies deprive us of the right to freely choose our fellow human beings, by abusing the egalitarian argument. This would be one of the last great deprivations of rights we are unaware of. Worse, we might be complicit in it.

But this book also presents Legitimate Preference as an extreme form of lucidity towards us all. Indeed, we would all be concerned by this disposition that our era has made shameful. The author shows the real social damage this situation causes: the aggravation of the detestation of the left and the right, the hypocrisy of self-righteousness, the degradation of the bond of trust between people. White people would really only have the choice between Legitimate Preference and its shameful version: Hypocritical Preference, to make their personal choices in the multiracial Western societies of the 21st century.

Legitimate Preference is at the crossroads between something so obvious that all white people practice it discreetly and a taboo so strong that these same white people will do anything to avoid being accused of racism.

Like a fall down the stairs, this book will lead you inexorably to exercise this relentless analysis of yourself.

Timothé Vorgens is the founder of a self-help community of Europeans: Les Braves. He has a master's degree in philosophy, is based in France, and has written several articles for American Renaissance magazine. Legitimate Preference is his first book.

WHO WANTS TO LOSE
THE RIGHT TO PREFER ?

Natiocracy

Revolution or "regime change"?

Events in Ukraine going back to "Euromaidan" in 2013 up to the full scale Russian invasion in February 2022 is a hotly contested topic, especially in avant-garde circles on the right.

The fact is the "Revolution of Dignity" not only paved the way for the medium-term eastward expansion of the European Union. Numerous Ukrainian nationalists and their diverse organisations have understood how to use this phase of political reorganisation for themselves – and to strengthen their position within society.

The political right in Ukraine made a strong comeback in recent years and has further bolstered its positions due to the war with Russia. Their worldview is based on one concept: Natiocracy. Its founder, Ukrainian veteran and political activist Mykola Sziborskyj, is the inspirational head of the Ukrainian right alongside the popular Stepan Bandera.

Natiocracy is a result of a detailed analysis of the political systems of his time. Prominent ideologies from democracy to fascism, but above all, an independent worldview for all Ukrainians. Sziborskyj's work is an exciting historical document and the indispensable key to understanding today's Ukraine and all of Eastern Europe.

The Ukrainian road to the 21st century is rocky, contradictory, and conflicting. Anyone who wants to educate themselves will have great help from the book of Mykola Sziborskyj.

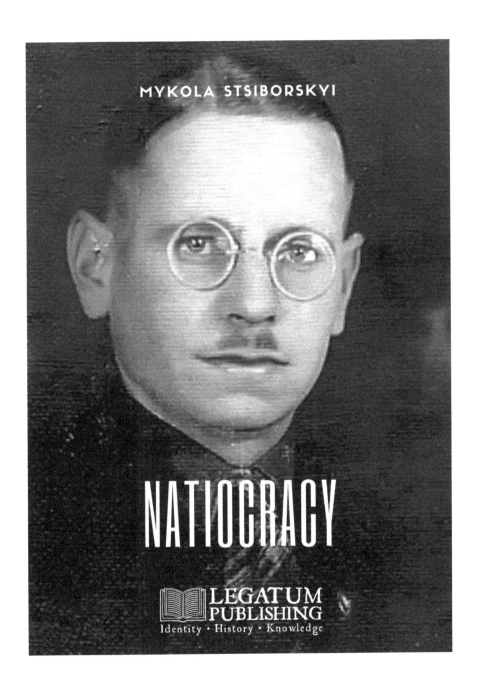

MYKOLA STSIBORSKYI

NATIOCRACY

LEGATUM
PUBLISHING
Identity · History · Knowledge

EuropePowerbrutal

"Everything begins the way it always does... With something on the head. And as I recapitulate it all, I somehow see Europe sparkling in the glasses."

EuropePowerbrutal is a kind of novel the political right in Germany has never seen before. Somewhere between the slum bars in the shadow of Cologne Cathedral, the underworld of Lyon, Viennese fraternity shacks and the gleaming marble of the Eternal City, a nameless narrator searches for the spirit of another Europe. Does this Europe really exist? In any case, this trip is so absurd, fast-paced, brutal and drunk, but also extremely funny that you can only do one thing: go along for the ride!

"As complex and almost asphalt-poetic as Hoewer describes small circles of passionate young people all over Europe and loudmouthed political good-for-nothings, on the other hand, one could almost think that the environment described really exists. But then the Federal Republic of Germany and other European countries would have to have gone completely to the dogs..." (Nils Wegner)

"Our parents put 'Storm of Steel' from Ernst Jünger in our hands and said: 'That's how it was back then'. We will put 'EuropePowerbrutal' in our children's hands and say: 'That's how we lived!'" (Volker Zierke)

EUROPE POWER BRUTAL

JOHN HOEWER